A complete grammar programme

Years 1 and 2

Raintree is an imprint of Capstone Global Library Limited, a company incorporated in England and Wales having its registered office at 7 Pilgrim Street, London, EC4V 6LB – Registered company number: 6695582

www.raintree.co.uk
myorders@raintree.co.uk

Devised and written by the Babcock LDP Primary English Team: Rebecca Cosgrave, Jenny Core, Sandra Murchison, Joy Simpson
Produced for Raintree by White-Thomson Publishing
Edited by Sonya Newland
Designed by Clare Nicholas
Proofread by Izzi Howell
Box and cover design by Richard Parker
Production by Helen McCreath
Originated by Capstone Global Library Ltd
Printed at Ashford Colour Press, Gosport, Hants

ISBN 978 1 4747 2032 8
19 18 17 16 15
10 9 8 7 6 5 4 3 2 1

British Library Cataloguing in Publication Data
A full catalogue record for this book is available from the British Library.

Acknowledgements
All photographs provided by Capstone Global Library

Contents

The USB stick features PDFs of books to be used in the teaching activities.
To access them, please enter the following password: Raintree

Foreword

With recent changes in the National Curriculum, and the introduction of new tests for primary children, grammar is once more at the forefront of teachers' thinking. Grammar has had a chequered history in schools, and was largely abandoned in the 1960s and 1970s because many felt it served no obvious purpose in the curriculum. As a consequence, many teachers who are now responsible for teaching grammar did not learn grammar themselves at school. A contested history combined with a cadre of teachers who are often anxious about their subject knowledge means that the reintroduction of grammar risks being viewed as a curriculum imposition rather than a creative opportunity.

Learning about grammar is learning about language, and about how meaning is created through the choices we make. It should not be a dry, dull enterprise, characterised by labelling exercises and learning rules (which is how many of us who did do grammar at school remember it). Rather, it should be a way of looking at the way the English language works and the endless possibilities it gives us for making our communication powerful. After all, through writing we can cause revolutions, break hearts, capture moments of history and express our deepest feelings! Grammar teaching in the twenty-first century should be a creative, enjoyable element of learning – generating curiosity about our language and encouraging a playful approach to language. It should also give young learners the opportunities to experience rich and diverse texts, exploring the choices that writers make in creating their texts.

This programme very much reflects this twenty-first century approach to the teaching of grammar. It is closely focused on the requirements of the National Curriculum and rooted in classroom practice. It combines the need to assess pupils' learning of grammar and to monitor their progress with a host of practical activities, which give learners an opportunity to play with and explore language actively. Written by authors who are established experts in primary literacy practice, it guides teachers to manage pupils' learning through plentiful opportunities for practising and applying. At the same time, it will support teachers' grammatical subject knowledge, giving confidence in approaching unfamiliar grammar concepts. This is grammar that lives and breathes!

Professor Debra Myhill FAcSS
Pro-Vice-Chancellor: College of Social Sciences and International Studies
Exeter University

Introduction: Grammar in the National Curriculum

Over the last few years, increasing emphasis has been placed on grammar and punctuation in primary schools. In particular, the new primary curriculum for English contains specific requirements for the teaching of grammar and punctuation within each year group and the learning that pupils should be able to demonstrate at the end of each year/key stage. There are a number of issues surrounding teaching and learning within this area of the curriculum.

Challenges for teachers

The first difficulty for teachers is that progression within each grammatical element is not always clear. Certain elements are mentioned in some year groups but not in others – for example, the present perfect tense appears in Year 3 but is not referred to again. The introduction to the National Curriculum Grammar Appendix states that the content in earlier years should be revisited and reinforced in subsequent years, but how should teachers do this? How, for example, should learning about the past perfect be consolidated in Years 4, 5 and 6? Furthermore, what groundwork is necessary to prepare pupils for learning some of the terminology they will come across? The term 'adverb' appears at Year 2, but can teachers do anything in Year 1 to make understanding adverbs easier for Year 2 pupils?

Another challenge for anyone teaching grammar and punctuation is the amount of subject knowledge required to feel comfortable with the content of the curriculum when the elements being taught can be used in so many different ways. Providing pupils with a pattern of language is a useful way of helping them understand a structure and how it can be used for effect. However, the English language is so flexible – with words, phrases and clauses capable of being used in extremely sophisticated structures – that it can be difficult to select examples of language that are correct for the grammatical feature being taught, appropriate to the text type being studied and not simplified to such a degree that their effect in writing is lost.

Subject knowledge

One area of subject knowledge that teachers may find particularly difficult is that caused by the merging of the previously separate 'sentence level' and 'text structure' strands. Although sentence structure and cohesion are inextricably linked, they are often considered discretely in teaching and assessment. In the National Curriculum Appendix, elements such as adverbials appear in the sentence and text sections, so teachers need to clearly understand when adverbials are being used to expand information for the reader and when they are acting cohesively to tie a text together.

Teaching grammar

The primary curriculum intends that pupils should develop a deep and secure understanding of grammar, and teachers are encouraged to go beyond the content set out in the Appendix if they feel it is appropriate. To achieve this, teachers need to ensure that learning is robust and can be applied in a variety of ways; they must also have a clear understanding of which concepts their pupils have successfully grasped and whether or not it is appropriate to go beyond the stated content. It is only by talking to pupils about texts and about their own writing that it is possible to ascertain whether or not they have attained the level of understanding required. Ensuring that they know the relevant terminology is key to enabling them to discuss their writing.

How *No Nonsense Grammar* is organised

The *No Nonsense Grammar* programme is intended to address the above challenges for the primary teacher, and includes the following features:

- A subject knowledge section, which explains the basic grammatical elements and constructions as well as the punctuation and cohesion required by the National Curriculum.
- Progression charts within each of the strands required by the National Curriculum. These detail the year group/key stage where each grammatical feature and punctuation mark is introduced and expanded upon. It explains which aspects of grammar pupils may find difficult, elaborates on any subject knowledge that might be useful for teachers and considers what consolidation or preparation would be useful in the year groups where features are not mentioned. It ends by considering how teachers could go beyond the content of the National Curriculum. Cohesion and punctuation objectives are cross-referenced to strand areas where it is relevant to include them in teaching.
- Grammar and punctuation teaching for Year 1, Year 2, Years 3 and 4, and Years 5 and 6, linked to assessment criteria, which provides:
  - information on what needs to be taught within each strand
  - appropriate generic activities, differentiated for each year group/key stage and strand area (in many cases, these include consolidation from previous teaching). The activities for strands 5 and 6 are integrated into all four of the other strands, as punctuation and cohesion cannot be taught in isolation.
  - links to teaching and learning sequences that use authentic texts with good models of writing and real purposes for writing
  - links with visual, auditory and kinaesthetic methods of teaching, such as some of the physical activities suggested and the use of the Babcock LDP *Sentence Toolkit* (see below)
  - resources
  - assessment activities where appropriate, including key questions to elicit understanding.
- Assessment criteria that explain what mastering each year group/key stage looks like and what pupils should understand and be able to do.
- Diagnostic assessment activities linked to the assessment criteria and the end of key stage assessment framework.

Whilst the *No Nonsense Grammar* programme provides activities and resources to support teachers, grammar should always be taught in context. It is the tool we use to communicate meaning, and that meaning should always be part of the discussion during teaching. Ideally, teachers will adapt the activities included in the programme and use them with the texts being studied. Across the programme we have provided three examples of a teaching and learning sequence for literacy, which show how grammar teaching should be embedded in wider English teaching. More sequences like these can be found at www.babcock-education.co.uk/ldp/

The USB stick

Included in this pack is a USB stick containing the following additional resources: instructional videos; PDFs of the books used in the teaching activities; editable versions of all three books in the programme, including the teaching resources.

The *Sentence Toolkit*

The abstract nature of grammar can make it difficult for young pupils to understand. The *Sentence Toolkit* has been developed and provided with the *No Nonsense Grammar* programme to help teachers make grammar come alive in the classroom and develop pupils' awareness and understanding.

The diagram below exemplifies the 'learning dip' surrounding learning in grammar. Pupils should be able to move beyond the awareness of features towards a genuine understanding of how they can be used to communicate effectively in writing. Exposing pupils to the correct terminology is essential in developing their understanding; using it will help pupils explore and explain how the features are used and the effects they have created.

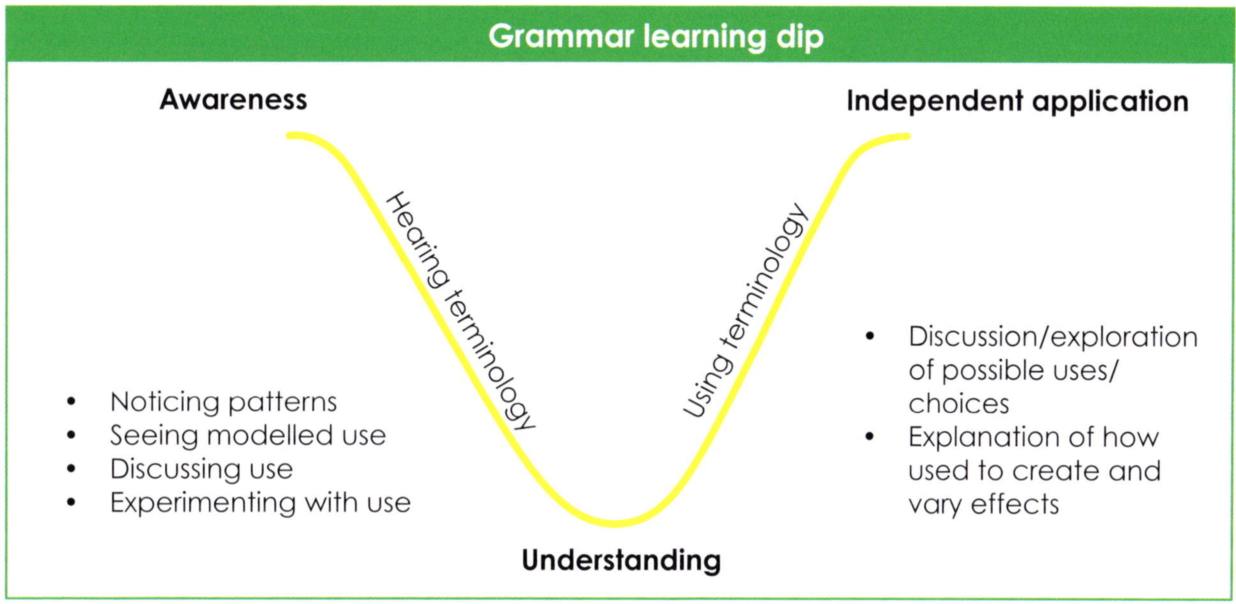

The bullet points on either side of the dip are also vital for progression, and the *Sentence Toolkit* provides a way to help pupils focus on the aspect of grammar being used, to understand its use and remember it when writing. It does this by linking the grammatical terminology to real-life objects and, where possible, provides analogies to aid pupils' understanding of how the different grammatical features work.

Each tool makes an association between the use of the tool in real life and a writing skill that can be viewed in a similar way. Each one has a specific name and purpose – for example, we can show pupils that a spanner is used to tighten bolts and join pieces of wood or metal together. In the same way, subordinating conjunctions can be used to join clauses together. Pupils can use this analogy to help them understand the terminology as well as the writing process and how it works. The visual clues provided and actions that can accompany the tools make this a multi-sensory approach to learning about grammar.

Full guidance on using the *Sentence Toolkit* can be found within the introduction to that document.

Subject knowledge and progression

Subject knowledge

Grammar is all about the patterns and rules in a language: how we put words, phrases and clauses together to make structures that communicate information clearly to our reader. Pupils have this grammatical knowledge in place from an early age, which enables them to understand structures they have not heard before and to know if what is communicated makes sense or not. Whether this grammar acquisition is innate or learned, young pupils pick up the grammatical structure of their language very quickly and their attempts at forming grammatical structures increasingly conform to the rules of their language.

By the time pupils go to school, they have a working knowledge of English grammar, but they are not always explicitly aware of the patterns and conventions that we use to speak and write. Spoken language does not usually have the clearly demarcated sections that are required in writing; if we want pupils to create – and punctuate – sentences, it is important that we help them understand what a 'sentence' is. In order to do that, we need to be clear ourselves about how sentences are formed.

Sentence building is a little like a modular construction kit. Every sentence contains at least one clause and each clause is made up of different grammatical elements, which we will refer to as **clause elements** in this text:

S – subject
V – verb
O – object (which can be direct or indirect)
A – adverbial
C – complement (adjective)/complement (noun phrase)

Complement is probably the least familiar clause element, and it does not have to be taught within the primary curriculum. However, it is important that teachers understand this common clause construction – for example, where the verb expresses a state of being: Fido is happy (SVC).

As with construction kits, each of these clause elements can occur in different shapes (structure) and sizes (length) but there are basic rules for fitting the components together. Word order (syntax) is a key factor, but there is a huge degree of flexibility in building a variety of structures to suit different purposes for writing.

We usually consider the default word order in English as being subject (S), verb (V), object (O) and this is frequently the order that pupils start off with in early writing:

The horse jumped the fence. The cat chased the mouse. Jack hit the ball.

However, we can combine these clause elements in a variety of ways. The most common sentence constructions are:

SV	The man slept.
SVO	The man painted the door.
SVC	The man was happy.
SVOC	The man painted the door yellow.
SVOO	The man gave the car a good clean. ('the car' is the indirect object, 'a good clean' is the direct object)

As a flexible clause element, adverbials can be added in various positions in these constructions:

SVA	The man slept peacefully.
ASV	Peacefully, the man slept.
SAV	The man peacefully slept.
ASVO	On Saturday, the man painted the door.
ASVOCA	Actually, the man painted the door yellow in under an hour.

In particular, using adverbials in different positions can create different effects for the reader by emphasising certain information in the sentence. When using adverbials in different positions, it is important to consider what punctuation is needed to make the meaning clear.

The sentences above are all simple – or single clause – structures. The clause element slots can be filled by single words or phrases. However, these clause element slots can also be filled by clauses. Usually sentences include a mix of words, phrases or clauses within each clause element slot, but the following sentences demonstrate how it is possible to use single words, phrases or clauses in these positions.

ASVO – with single words filling each clause element slot:

Excitedly,	Fido	chased	Tibbles.

ASVO – with phrases filling each clause element slot:

In excitement,	the playful dog Fido	started to chase	the tiny kitten.

ASVO – with clauses filling the A, S and O slots:

As he barked excitedly,	the playful dog belonging to Mr Smith	started to chase	the tiny kitten, which mewed in fear.

In the last example, an adverbial clause fills the adverbial slot, while relative clauses post-modify the nouns in the subject and object positions.

Some of the terminology in the National Curriculum links directly to these clause elements: verb (Y2), adverbial (Y3/4), subject (Y5/6), object (Y5/6). Other terminology covers the grammatical constructions that fill these element slots: noun/noun phrase, adverb (Y2), relative clause (Y5). The challenge for teachers is to help pupils to:

- understand how to fill these clause element slots
- develop a terminology for talking about the constructions
- improve their writing through varying and manipulating the component parts of the sentence, considering the effects they are creating.

Understanding how words, phrases and clauses fit together empowers pupils to communicate their ideas in speech and writing. They can experiment with different constructions and decide how effective and appropriate they are in different situations. This is, therefore, inextricably linked with the teaching of different genres and text types.

Progression

The following subject knowledge sections deal with different grammatical features and progression within each strand of the National Curriculum. They highlight potentially tricky aspects of grammar and elaborate on subject knowledge that teachers may find useful. They also consider useful areas of consolidation in the year groups where features are not mentioned, and offer suggestions for how to go beyond the content outlined in the National Curriculum. In particular, the 'tricky bit' sections will help teachers understand any awkward or confusing structures in the texts they are using, enabling them to choose appropriate models for teaching and learning.

In the following charts, the curriculum requirements are shown in blue, while terminology for pupils is indicated in red. Relevant *Sentence Toolkit* images are included in each of the sections. Each curriculum objective and associated terminology appears in the year group/key stage where it should be introduced. It is important that concepts are regularly revisited after initial teaching and terminology is consistently used in all year groups after it has been introduced. Although cohesion and punctuation strands have their own subject knowledge and progression charts, these are both cross-referenced in other strands where they can be incorporated into teaching.

Pupils often write as they speak – for example, using vocabulary such as 'like' and 'sort of'. Within the National Curriculum, there is an increased focus on pupils using Standard English in their speaking and writing. That task is challenging when another dialect is spoken outside school by family, friends, within the community and in popular media. While we should value the rich variation in language that a local dialect provides, it is important that pupils understand that Standard English is necessary for communicating with people outside their dialect area and for specific formal purposes. Once they understand that Standard English is a dialect used for a specific purpose, they have a choice: knowledge of two different ways of communicating and understanding the appropriate time and place for each. The Standard English requirements in the curriculum have been incorporated into the most relevant chart below.

Strand 1: Different ways to construct sentences

Sentences can be simple (single clause) structures, or they can be built up to include two or more (multi) clauses. These can be created through co-ordination or subordination. Sentences also occur in different types: statement, question, command and explanation. Before pupils come into Year 1, they will be encouraged to read and write simple sentences, using phonically decodable and common 'tricky' words. Talking about sentences and what information, words and punctuation marks they contain will help prepare pupils for the writing requirements in Year 1.

Strand 1a: Simple sentences

All full sentences in English must contain a verb, so constructing a simple sentence in its most basic form will require a subject and a verb (SV). The subject position in a sentence is filled by a noun or noun phrase. The verb position may contain a simple verb form, which will consist of one word, or a verb phrase, in which auxiliary verbs are used with a main noun. For example: *The small boy ate*. (noun phrase + present simple verb) or *The small boy was eating*. (noun phrase + past progressive)

You can add to this basic simple sentence structure with objects, complements and adverbials. For example: *The small boy was eating an apple noisily.* (SVOA)

When encouraging pupils to create sentences, it is vital to talk about what information is contained in the sentence and what sense it will make for the reader. Questions around sentences will be included in the year/key stage teaching and learning sections.

	Y1	Y2	Y3/4	Y5/6
National Curriculum content: Constructing a simple sentence (or single-clause sentence)	How **words** can combine to make **sentences**. Introduction to capital letters, full stops … to demarcate **sentences**. Capital letters for names and for the personal **pronoun**. word sentence letter capital letter punctuation full stop Sequencing **sentences** to form short narratives.			
Preparation or consolidation		As pupils become more comfortable with the process of writing, help them understand how to extend sentences to provide additional detail. Later sections will explain how this is done, but the process of oral rehearsal, questioning about the information included and what sense is made for the reader is as important in Y6 as it is in Y1. Manipulating the order of the clause elements to create different effects is a focus for discussion – for example, different positions of adverbials, subject-verb inversion. Linking to ideas of composition, pupils will need to know when it is appropriate or desirable to use simple sentences in their writing, to match the text type or create particular effects.		
Tricky bits	Teachers often ask how they can help pupils understand where to place full stops. Before dealing with punctuation, however, pupils must have some understanding of what a sentence is. One of the most important steps in Y1 learning is for pupils to be able to orally compose a sentence and talk about sentences. To use the required terminology *sentence*, they need to develop some concept of what a sentence is and what information it contains (without requiring the terminology covered above: SVOAC). First of all, pupils need to understand that a sentence tells the reader about something that is happening or what something is like. Starting with a basic sentence consisting of just a subject and a verb (e.g. *Jack fell*), ask pupils 'Who fell?' or 'What happened?/ What did Jack do?' to get them used to the idea that a sentence is about someone or something who either *does*, *has* or *is* something. Notice the final punctuation and discuss it. Act out some of the sentences and have an action for the full stop. Sometimes in a sentence, someone is affected by the action or information is given about where, when or how it is happening, so you might need to discuss the object of the sentence or the adverbials used, using language pupils can understand. It is the discussion that is important, so they get an idea of what sort of information is included in a sentence. Encourage them to create their own verbal sentences, discuss what they contain and put in a piece of final punctuation with an action. Then, when they start to write, the concept of sentences and full stops will be familiar to them.			

Going beyond in Y1	Much of the talk in Y1 will centre on actions that are 'done'. It is important not to refer to verbs only as 'doing words', as this will confuse pupils when they come across verbs such as *be*, *seem* and *have*, but questions will certainly be based on what someone is doing in the sentence. Moving beyond this involves discussing sentences where verbs fit into the 'having' or 'state of being' sense (e.g. *Maisie has a cold* or *Teddy is happy*). Pupils need to understand that these types of verbs (e.g. *has* and *is*) fill the same slot in the sentence as a word that can be said to have been 'done'.

Strand 1b: Co-ordination and subordination

Compound sentences are formed when two clauses are joined using a co-ordinating conjunction. Each clause will contain a verb or verb phrase and, although the clauses may not be the same length or contain exactly the same clause elements, they are considered grammatically equal – one is no more important than the other. For example: *Jack played on the slide and Sam climbed the tree*.

If the subject is the same in both clauses, we often omit the subject in the second clause. For example: *Dad washed the car and mowed the lawn*.

The main co-ordinating conjunctions are: *and*, *but*, *or*, *(and) then*, *yet* and *nor*. In a compound sentence, the conjunction always remains between the two clauses. Even if the clauses can be put in a different order the position of the conjunction does not change – it is not 'fixed' to either clause, but merely links the two together.

Complex sentences also contain two or more clauses, but here one is the main clause and additional clauses are subordinate. A subordinate clause cannot stand on its own as a sentence. Sometimes subordinate clauses may start a sentence; sometimes they may be positioned at the end of a sentence and sometimes they may be embedded within the sentence.

There are different types of subordinate clause: adverbial, relative and nominal. Adverbial clauses fill an adverbial slot in a sentence, relative clauses extend noun phrases and nominal clauses usually occur in subject or object positions in a sentence (see Appendix for further information).

When subordination is first taught to pupils the focus is on adverbial clauses, which are introduced with subordinating conjunctions such as *because*, *when*, *after*, *before*, *if*, *as*, *while*. These clauses can be placed in different positions within a sentence, and pupils will need to experiment with manipulation to investigate the different effects that can be created. For example:

- ***When he arrived****, the lights were already on.*
- *The lights were already on* ***when he arrived****.*

It is important that pupils understand how to demarcate clauses with punctuation. If the subordinate clause starts the sentence, a comma is required to demarcate the two clauses. If the main clause starts the sentence, the comma is optional. Pupils should consider whether it is needed to aid clarity and sense for their reader. If the clause is embedded, it will need to be enclosed in commas. For example: *She danced,* ***as she always had done****, to please the audience.*

Although not mentioned in the curriculum, an effective way of creating subordinate clauses involves the use of non-finite structures. In the chart below, these appear in the 'Going beyond' section and further detail is provided in the Appendix. If using the *Sentence Toolkit*, three additional spanners are provided for these structures.

	Y1	Y2	Y3/4	Y5/6
National Curriculum content: Co-ordination and subordination	Joining **words** and joining **clauses** using *and*. Introduction to capital letters, full stops … to demarcate **sentences**. sentence capital letter punctuation full stop	**Subordination** (using *when*, *if*, *that*, *because*) and **co-ordination** (using *or*, *and*, *but*). compound verb Use of capital letters, full stops … to demarcate **sentences**.	Expressing time, place and cause using **conjunctions** (for example, *when*, *before*, *after*, *while*, *so*, *because*). conjunction clause subordinate clause Use of commas after **fronted adverbials** (where these are fronted adverbial clauses).	Use of the semi-colon, colon and dash to mark the boundary between independent **clauses** (for example, *It's raining; I'm fed up*). semi-colon colon dash Use of commas to clarify meaning or avoid **ambiguity**. ambiguity **Brackets**, **dashes** or commas to indicate **parenthesis**. parenthesis bracket dash The difference between structures typical of informal and formal speech, and writing.
Preparation or consolidation	Talking about the meanings of *because* and *when*. Use these in oral sentences.	Extending oral sentences – giving reasons or talking about timing of actions: *Before we … After he …* Making sure pupils understand the meanings of conjunctions.	Using an increasingly wide range of conjunctions to create complex (multi-clause) sentences. Understanding that commas need to be used in a list of clauses. Making sure pupils understand the meanings of conjunctions. Starting to manipulate clauses to create effects. Explaining how simple, compound and complex structures are used in texts (e.g. subordination for building up description; simple for building suspense).	Making sure pupils understand the meanings of conjunctions. Continuing to develop pupils' understanding around co-ordination as well as subordination. Using compound sentences for effect. Understanding how manipulation of clauses can add to effectiveness and variation in writing. Developing understanding around the appropriateness and effectiveness of simple, compound and complex structures in different text types.

	Y1	Y2	Y3/4	Y5/6
Tricky bits	Understanding the meaning of the conjunctions used. Understanding that, although these structures occur in a 'stream' in speech, it is important not to use too many clauses in one sentence. Encourage pupils to only join two (maximum three) sentences together with *and* before they add their full stop.	Understanding the difference between co-ordination and subordination and finding clear, straightforward examples from texts. Using the different *Toolkit* tools can help distinguish compound and complex sentences. The different ways in which *that* can be used: relative, adverbial and nominal clauses (see Appendix). This is not a focus of teaching in Y2, but it is necessary for teachers to understand the differences, particularly when choosing examples to model. Pupils may think that a subordinate clause can stand on its own as a sentence. Lots of modelling and talk around the sense of these should help them understand the need for both subordinate and main clauses.	Linking with verb work to help pupils understand that each clause will contain a verb. Understanding when words are acting as a conjunction and when they are acting as a preposition. Some words can be either and the job they are doing will depend on which words follow. For example: *He knew he was injured because he was bleeding.* (*because* is a conjunction as it introduces a clause) *He knew he was injured because of the blood.* (*because of the blood* is a prepositional phrase; no verb is included, only preposition + noun phrase). When pupils start to understand conjunctions and clauses, they may be confused by the different types of subordinate clause. They will need to know that some are adverbial clauses, which can be used to add information (e.g. how, where, when, why), but others are not and do not fit the pattern of manipulation. For example, in reported speech, where *that* introduces a nominal clause.	Developing understanding around which subordinate structures are relative clauses and which are adverbial clauses. Understanding how to use a range of punctuation marks appropriately. As knowledge of subordination and alternative punctuation increases, it can be difficult for pupils to make appropriate choices. Overuse of semi-colons, colons and dashes should be avoided and pupils should be encouraged to think about a mix of subordinate clauses, with a variety of word orders: • adverbial clauses starting with main clause • adverbial clauses starting with subordinate clause • non-finite clauses starting with main clause • non-finite clauses starting with subordinate clause • multi-clause structures (e.g. power of three, mix of compound and complex).

	Y1	Y2	Y3/4	Y5/6
Tricky bits (continued)			There will be two verbs in these sentences, but manipulation of the clauses does not work in the same way as an adverbial clause because the nominal clause is filling the object position in the sentence. For example: *He knew that she would be late*. We can replace the clause with a pronoun (*He knew this*.) The structure here is SVO.	
Going beyond	Some pupils may start to use *because*, *when* and *but* in their writing.	Starting to introduce a wider range of conjunctions and encourage pupils to use these orally and in writing.	Manipulation of clauses. Starting sentences with non-finite present participles (*-ing*).	Non-finite structures using both present and past participles and the infinitive. Manipulation of these to consider the most appropriate/effective construction. Hybrid multi-clause constructions (e.g. mixing compound and complex). Develop clauses using the power of three (e.g. *Singing loudly, shouting jokes and giggling hysterically, they annoyed everyone on the train.*)

Strand 1c: Sentence types

There are four different sentence types in English:

- **Statements** provide some information to the reader. We can describe these to pupils as 'telling' us something. Most sentences fall into this category and pupils need to know that they are punctuated with a full stop.
- **Questions** ask something. These sentences often start with the words *What, When, Where, Who, Why* or *How*, but they can also be formed in different ways, such as beginning with a modal verb, where a pronoun or noun splits the auxiliary verb and the main verb (***Could*** *we* ***meet*** *on Thursday?*) or final question tags (*He has arrived,* ***hasn't he****?*). They end with a question mark.

- **Commands** order somebody to do something and end in a full stop. The command structure can be used flexibly to deliver an order (*Put it there.*), but also to give advice (*Take care not to rip the paper.*), warn somebody (*Look out for the uneven pavement.*) or issue an invitation (*Come and see us soon.*) They can be used in a polite way, with *please*, to request rather than order (*Please sit down.*)
- **Exclamations** indicate an element of excitement or emphasis and end with an exclamation mark. A complete exclamatory sentence will begin with *What* or *How* (*What a great party that was!; How nice to meet you again!*) In dialogue, exclamation marks are often used with words or phrases to express strong feelings or emotions: these are called interjections (*Amazing!, Wow!, Not again!*)

Once pupils have understood these structures, they should be encouraged to use them in their writing where appropriate.

	Y1	**Y2**	**Y3/4**	**Y5/6**
National Curriculum content: Sentence types	Introduction to capital letters, full stops, question marks and exclamation marks to demarcate **sentences**. Capital letters for names and for the personal **pronoun**. letter capital letter punctuation full stop question mark exclamation mark	How the grammatical patterns in a sentence indicate its function as a **statement, question, exclamation** or **command**. Use of capital letters, full stops, question marks and exclamation marks to demarcate **sentences**. statement question exclamation command	Introduction to inverted commas to **punctuate** direct speech. Use of inverted commas and other **punctuation** to indicate direct speech (for example, a comma after the reporting clause; end punctuation within inverted commas: *The conductor shouted, 'Sit down!'*) direct speech inverted commas (or speech marks)	The difference between structures typical of informal speech and structures appropriate for formal speech and writing (for example, the use of question tags: *He's your friend, isn't he?*).
Preparation or consolidation	Developing talk around questions, commands and exclamations. 'Noticing' the different punctuation marks used for questions and exclamations.	Different ways of forming questions. Some ways are more appropriate for speech: • starting with *What, When, Where, Who, Why, How* • starting with a verb phrase that is split by a noun/pronoun: *Is he playing today? Can we have a biscuit? Have you seen it? Did you know …?*	Developing a range of uses for different sentence types in different text types (e.g. questions in information texts). Collecting interjections to use in exclamatory speech, but talking about how these are not full sentences.	Developing a range of uses for different sentence types in different text types, including hybrid texts. Thinking about the appropriateness of these to the purpose/audience. Linking sentence types in texts to the levels of formality required. Link with Standard English. Making links with modal verbs and apostrophes for contractions when writing dialogue.

	Y1	Y2	Y3/4	Y5/6
Tricky bits		Understanding that the grammatical pattern is different in different sentence types. Understanding the imperative verb in commands. This is the same for each grammatical person, so it does not change in the third person singular like the verb in a statement does. Also there is no subject in a command (although *you* is implied). Finding opportunities to use the different sentence types. Link to dialogue in fiction, instructional writing and questions in information texts. True exclamatory sentences are rare – most are interjections.	Understanding that dialogue in stories reflects natural speech. Although the different sentence types will all be present, they are not always going to occur in full sentences.	Getting the balance right in texts: • not too many questions in a persuasive piece of writing • using a mix of different sentence types in dialogue, but with a balance of dialogue and narrative • developing instructional writing through blending the imperative voice with authoritative and advisory adverbials. Although we usually create complex sentences with statements, other sentence types can also contain more than one clause. For example, a command main clause can be preceded by a subordinate clause: *After you have finished the dishes, phone your mother.*
Going beyond		How to give advice in commands.	Developing an authoritative voice in commands.	Make links with cohesion to show how substitution and ellipses (omission) are used in dialogue. This is important to support discussion about appropriate levels of formality and how Standard English is adapted in day-to-day speech.

Strand 2: Nouns and noun phrases

Nouns and noun phrases describe people, objects and places. They fill the subject and object slots in sentences (***The policeman*** *arrested* ***the burglar***. SVO). They can also occur in complement positions (***My nephew*** *became* ***a fireman***. SVC). They can also be used in prepositional phrases, which means that they often occur in adverbial phrases (***The castle*** *stood on* ***a rocky outcrop***. SVA). Sometimes nouns can stand alone in a sentence. For example:

- **Suzie** won the race. (Proper nouns can stand alone.)
- **Sunflowers** can grow very tall. (Many plural nouns can stand alone.)
- **Wool** is useful for making warm clothes. (Mass nouns often stand alone.)
- **History** is interesting. (Many uncount nouns – qualities, substances, processes and topics – can stand alone.)

However, in other situations more than one word is needed to fill the subject or object slot, so a noun phrase must be used. The main noun appears as the head of a noun phrase, but other words can be added before or after the main noun to create the phrase. A complete noun phrase can always be substituted by a pronoun. For example:

- ***The smiling man in the moon*** *disappeared behind a cloud.*
- ***He*** *disappeared behind a cloud.*

Developing a noun phrase by adding words before the main noun

When pupils start to write, they tend to use basic noun phrases with only the determiners *a*/*an* or *the* in front of the noun; they may want to write more, but they do not know how to express these additional ideas. It is important to encourage pupils to describe objects, people and places orally at an early stage so that they get used to adding this detail and can apply it in their writing later on.

Determiners, adverbs and adjectives can be placed in front of the head noun. Determiners help define the noun, adjectives are used to describe a noun and adverbs modify the adjective (*my perfectly beautiful necklace*). One or more adjectives can be used before a noun to add detail and build up a noun phrase (*my bright silver necklace*). The following table provides examples of these word classes. You can, of course, use more than one adjective and words do not have to be selected from every column (*my first silver necklace*).

Determiner	Adverb	Adjective	Main noun
a, an, the, this, that, these, those, some, many, my, your, her, our, several, few, last, next, first, fifth, seven, ten	slightly very extremely really exceedingly perfectly surprisingly rather quite considerably	beautiful bright annoying terrifying mysterious wonderful silver famous unsettling peaceful	dream necklace

Developing a noun phrase by adding words after the main noun

There are two ways to develop the noun phrase by adding detail after the head noun – by using a prepositional phrase or by using a relative clause.

Prepositional phrases can make writing more efficient. For example:

A cat was sheltering under the bush. It was drenched and shivering.
***The cat under the bush** was drenched and shivering.*

We know that the emboldened section is the noun phrase because it can be replaced with the pronoun *It*. (For more about prepositional phrases, see Appendix.)

Like prepositional phrases, relative clauses allow you to be more efficient when adding detail to sentences. Relative clauses are introduced by relative pronouns:

Relative pronoun	Example (noun phrase emboldened)
who	***My father, who was relaxing in the garden,** didn't hear a thing.*
whom	***Her grandson, whom she doted on,** was a funny boy.*
which	***Their car, which they had only just bought,** broke down.*
that	***The journalist that had written the story** won a prize.*
where	***The town where they lived** was always in the news.*

Relative pronouns refer to a person or object that has already been mentioned, but they also act like conjunctions joining clauses. Note that sometimes relative clauses are written without the relative pronoun, particularly *that*. For example: *The main reason they came was the football.*

When the clause contains additional information, it is enclosed in commas (referred to as a 'non-restrictive' or 'non-defining' clause). If the clause identifies the noun, commas are not used and the clause is said to be 'restrictive' or 'defining'. For example:

*My sister, **who lives in Sweden**, phoned me yesterday.*
The relative clause provides additional information about my sister: where she lives.

*My sister **who lives in Sweden** phoned me yesterday.*
The relative clause identifies which sister phoned me – the one that lives in Sweden.

National Curriculum content: Nouns and noun phrases	Y1	Y2	Y3/4	Y5/6
	Regular **plural noun suffixes** *-s* or *-es* (for example, *dog, dogs; wish, wishes*), including the effects of these suffixes on the meaning of the noun. How the **prefix** *un-* changes the meaning of **verbs** and **adjectives** (negation, for example, *unkind*, or *undoing: untie the boat*). singular plural	Formation of **nouns** using **suffixes** such as *-ness, -er* and by compounding (for example, *whiteboard, superman*). Formation of **adjectives** using **suffixes** such as *-ful, -less*. Use of the **suffixes** *-er, -est* in **adjectives**. Expanded **noun phrases** for description and specification (for example, *the blue butterfly, plain flour, the man in the moon*). noun noun phrase compound adjective suffix Commas to separate items in a list. comma **Apostrophes** to mark singular possession in nouns (for example, *the girl's name*). apostrophe	Formation of **nouns** using a range of **prefixes** (for example *super-, anti-, auto-*). **Word families** based on common **words**, showing how words are related in form and meaning (for example, *solve, solution, solver, dissolve, insoluble*). word family Use of the **forms** *a* or *an* according to whether the next **word** begins with a **consonant** or a **vowel** (for example, ***a** rock, **an** open box*). The grammatical difference between **plural** and **possessive** *-s*. **Apostrophes** to mark singular and **plural** possession (for example, *the girl's name, the girls' names*). Noun phrases expanded by the addition of modifying adjectives, nouns and prepositional phrases (for example, *the teacher expanded to the strict maths teacher with curly hair*). determiner pronoun possessive pronoun preposition prefix consonant vowel	**Relative clauses** beginning with *who, which, where, when, whose, that*, or an omitted relative pronoun. Use of commas to clarify meaning or avoid ambiguity. How words are related by meaning as synonyms and antonyms (for example, *big, large, little*). relative pronoun relative clause subject object synonym antonym cohesion How hyphens can be used to avoid ambiguity (for example, *man eating shark* versus *man-eating shark*, or *recover* versus *re-cover*). hyphen (Although *hyphen* is terminology in Y6, this punctuation mark will be used in word work and writing from Y2 onwards).

	Y1	Y2	Y3/4	Y5/6
National Curriculum content: Nouns and noun phrases (continued)			Appropriate choice of **pronoun** or **noun** within and across **sentences** to aid cohesion and avoid repetition. pronoun possessive pronoun	
Preparation or consolidation	Talking about the *who* and *what* in sentences. Pupils need to understand where noun phrases can be placed – particularly subject and object positions. Oral development of noun phrase by adding adjectives. Starting to use adjectives in writing. Using the 'tricky word' determiners from phonics teaching in oral and written sentences. Talking about how these are useful to start a description of someone or something instead of just *a* or *the*. Talking about and modelling the use of pronouns to replace a noun to avoid repeating it (link with cohesion).	Developing noun phrase expansion using prepositional phrases (e.g. *the man in the moon*), in preparation for Y3/4 use of prepositions. Looking at how all of a noun phrase can be replaced with a pronoun, to consolidate knowledge of subject/object *who* or *what* in a sentence. Modelling and encouraging correct use of *a* and *an* in preparation for Y3/4. Consolidating the use of 'tricky word' determiners and introducing others to vary the start of noun phrases.	Understanding that determiners are part of the noun phrase and the different types that can be used. Learning how to create prepositional phrases that post-modify nouns. Developing noun-phrase expansion for appropriateness and effectiveness in writing. Looking at precise nouns for succinctness and accuracy. Linking work on punctuation for speech to reported speech, which uses a nominal clause, introduced by *that*, to fill the object position in a sentence. For example: *Michael said that he was not interested.* (Pupils do not need to know the term *nominal clause*.)	Continuing to work on correct subject and object pronouns in speech (where Standard English is required) and writing. Choice of noun/noun phrase will also be important when writing more formal texts. Although the only development of noun phrase here is with relative clauses, pre-modification can also be developed using adverbs. Consolidating work on not using noun phrases as a formula, but considering their effect on the reader. Consolidating work on who or what the sentence is about (the subject) and who or what is affected in a sentence (the object). This will lead into work on passive verbs.

	Y1	Y2	Y3/4	Y5/6
Tricky bits	Using the correct pronoun to replace a noun. Encourage the correct use of Standard English subject and object pronouns. For example, look at the sentence, *Me and Dan like them*. This is incorrect because the object pronoun (*me*) is used in the subject position instead of the subject pronoun (*I*).	Distinguishing between when description is appropriate and when nouns should be more precise. Understanding what suffixes mean as well as how to form the adjective. Encourage the correct use of Standard English subject and object pronouns. Understanding that commas can separate items in a list of words or phrases, which can be adjectives or nouns.	Understanding the difference between the Standard English subject and object pronouns and how this varies from the dialect they may use at home. Understanding that a possessive pronoun replaces the noun phrase (e.g. *mine*), whereas a determiner is placed at the start of the noun phrase (e.g. *my*). Determiners are difficult for EAL pupils who do not use these in their first language.	Using synonyms to aid cohesion in a text. Pupils need to understand that using synonyms (and antonyms), plus other closely related vocabulary, varies their writing, but also helps the text make sense for their reader. (Link with cohesion.) Examples: Synonyms: *horse, nag* Near synonyms: *pony, stallion* Antonyms: *It was the best of times, it was the worst of times …* Connected vocabulary: *lion, cat, mane, animal, pride*
Going beyond	Using the term *adjective*. Introduce using adjectives orally and in writing to describe nouns in an SVC structure. • *Jim was happy.* • *Tiger was soft and cuddly.*	Although *hyphen* is terminology in Y6, this punctuation mark will be used in word work and writing from Y2 onwards. Introduce and develop adjectives and adjectival phrases in complementation slots. Use hyphenated adjectives, simple modifiers (e.g. *very*) and compound structures. • *The squirrel was* ***bushy tailed****.* • *The squirrel was* ***very fluffy****.* • *The squirrel was* ***bright-eyed and bushy tailed****.* Compare these structures with pre-modified nouns to show pupils how they can transform descriptions: • *The bushy-tailed squirrel …*	Developing adjectival phrases in complement slots using adverbial modifiers: • *The princess was* ***understandably upset****.* • *These cakes are* ***exceedingly good****.* • *He seems* ***remarkably cheerful****.*	Developing adjectival phrases in complement slots using the power of three: • *The scout was* ***quick-thinking, extremely brave and surprisingly calm****.* Developing punctuation use in relative clauses.

Strand 3: Adverbials

Adverbials are used for many different reasons. Primary pupils begin by using them to provide more information about how, where or when something happened, moving onto 'why' once they have grasped the concept.

- *The princess smiled smugly*. (how/manner using an adverb)
- *The pupils left the room in silence*. (how/manner using an adverbial phrase)
- *The fish swam through the coral like a dart*. (how/manner using an adverbial phrase that is a simile)
- *The dragon flew beyond the snow-capped mountains*. (where/direction)
- *The dragon waited in his cave*. (where/position)
- *The rider reached his destination by the end of the day*. (when/time)
- *The maid collected water every day*. (frequency/time)
- *The postman walked for six hours*. (duration/time)

Adverbials can often be placed in different positions within a sentence, but some positions sound better than others – they flow more naturally. Sometimes we alter the positions to create a specific effect:

- *Mysteriously, the ship disappeared into the fog.*
- *The ship disappeared mysteriously into the fog.*
- *The ship disappeared into the fog, mysteriously.*
- *Into the fog, the ship mysteriously disappeared.*

One particularly effective aspect of this flexibility when using adverbials is the possibility of inverting subject and object in a sentence that starts with an adverbial of place:

- *Under the thick, green growth lurked the crocodile.*
- *Over the hills, through the forests and beyond the river flew the silver dragon.*

Adverbials are also used to connect ideas in a text (so acting cohesively). They can have the following functions:

- addition: *also, furthermore, moreover, in addition*
- opposition: *however, nevertheless, on the other hand*
- reinforcing: *besides, anyway, after all*
- explaining: *for example, in other words, that is to say*
- listing: *first(ly), first of all, finally*
- indicating result: *therefore, consequently, as a result*
- focusing: *only, merely, simply, especially, just*

The table below explains some of the terminology associated with adverbials.
This terminology is not required in the National Curriculum but is included to support teachers' understanding.

Adjuncts	• Some adverbials are used to provide information to the reader that is not contained in the subject, verb, object or complement. These are called *adjuncts* and are integral to the sentence. • They can be single words (*quickly*, *home*, *almost*, *away*, *curiously*), phrases (*down the street*, *at the end of the day*, *extremely angrily*, *because of the rain*) or clauses (*when he left the station*, *as you climb the cliff*, *if the doctor can see me*). • Commas are optional when adverbials are used for adding information and their use depends on clarity and effect for the reader. However, fronted adverbials – whether words, phrases or clauses – are usually demarcated with commas.
Conjuncts	• Some adverbials have a cohesive function, connecting different parts of the text – for example linking a new sentence to a previous sentence or paragraph. These are called *conjuncts* (or *connecting adverbs*) and are usually placed at, or near, the beginning of the sentence. (These used to be referred to in some documents as *connectives*.) • Conjuncts are usually individual words (*first*, *next*, *finally*, *meanwhile*, *furthermore*, *alternatively*) or phrases (*in the same way*, *on the other hand*, *for example*, *in the meantime*). • When adverbials are used to connect in this way, they always require a comma for demarcation.
Disjuncts	• The third type of adverbial is called a *disjunct*. These provide information about the speaker's/writer's beliefs or feelings. • Disjuncts can be words (*seriously*, *personally*, *obviously*, *understandably*), phrases (*of course*, *to be blunt*, *very wisely*, *in my opinion*) or clauses (*it was understandable*, *which is clearly wrong*, *I'm telling you confidentially*, *what is certain*). • These require commas to demarcate them from the rest of the sentence.

	Y1	Y2	Y3/4	Y5/6
National Curriculum content: Adverbials		Use of *-ly* in Standard English to turn adjectives into **adverbs**. adverb	Expressing time, place and cause using **adverbs** (for example, *then*, *next*, *soon*, *therefore*), or **prepositions** (for example, *before*, *after*, *during*, *in*, *because of*). **Fronted adverbials** (for example, *Later that day, I heard the bad news.*) adverb preposition adverbial Use of commas after **fronted adverbials**.	Indicating degrees of possibility using **adverbs** (for example, *perhaps*, *surely*). Devices to build **cohesion** within a paragraph (for example, *then*, *after that*, *this*, *firstly*). Linking ideas across paragraphs using **adverbials** of time (for example, *later*), place (for example, *nearby*) and number (for example, *secondly*). Linking ideas across paragraphs using a wider range of **cohesive devices**. Grammatical connections (for example, the use of **adverbials** such as *on the other hand*, *in contrast*, or *as a consequence*). cohesion
Preparation or consolidation	Understanding *how*, *where*, *when* in sentences.	Understanding *how* and *when* in sentences to add information for reader. Understanding that the term *adverb* refers to a single word that fills the adverbial slot. This will prepare pupils for work on phrases and clauses in Y3/4.	Any work on using adverbials cohesively will be preparation for Y5/6.	Consolidating adverbs/ adverbial phrases/ adverbial clauses in preparation for the grammar and punctuation test.

	Y1	Y2	Y3/4	Y5/6
Tricky bits	Understanding how to express position and time. Pupils do not need to know the term, but they should understand the meanings of many common prepositions (e.g. *between*, *on top of*, *afterwards*, *through*, *across*).	Although many adverbs end in *-ly*, several common ones do not. Pupils will be using words such as *now*, *soon*, *away*, *almost*, *off*, *fast* – and they should understand that these also give information about when, where or how.	In Y3, the term *adverb* appears again. Although the grammar for this year group covers prepositions (which will introduce phrases) and subordinate (adverbial) clauses, *adverbial* is not terminology for pupils until Y4. Using prepositions, pupils will create prepositional phrases for adverbial slots; these will occur in different positions (e.g. *The haunting cry drifted* ***through the forest. Through the forest****, the haunting cry drifted*.) Using conjunctions, pupils will create subordinate clauses for the adverbial slots in complex sentences and experiment with manipulating these. (e.g. *He was tired* ***when he stopped. When he stopped****, he was tired*.) The confusion for pupils in Y3 is that many prepositions are also conjunctions. Pupils should understand when the adverbial is a phrase or a clause: • *I couldn't see* ***because of my tears***. (adverbial phrase) • *I couldn't see* ***because I had been crying***. (adverbial clause)	Pupils will be exposed to a wider range of connecting adverbials, which are used for different purposes in different text types. They may be unsure which conjunct to use in which text type and end up making inappropriate choices – for example, using more formal conjuncts (connecting adverbs) used for non-fiction texts (*furthermore*, *nevertheless*, *moreover*) inappropriately in fiction.

	Y1	Y2	Y3/4	Y5/6
Tricky bits (continued)			Pupils may not realise that similes are preposition/ adverbial phrases, introduced by the preposition *like* and prepositional phrase *as … as*. In Y4, teaching takes places around fronted adverbials, which could be single words, phrases or clauses. All will need commas to demarcate them. • ***Slowly****, he swam to the surface.* • ***Like a dolphin****, he swam to the surface.* • ***When he could no longer hold his breath****, he swam to the surface.*	
Going beyond		Encouraging pupils to use prepositional phrases to give information about how, where and when an action is taking place. (They do not need the terminology *preposition* at this stage.) Talking about how similes show *how* something is happening.	Distinguishing adverbial phrases from adverbial clauses. Making links with cohesion when fronted adverbials are conjuncts (connecting adverbs). Where examples are provided in texts, introduce subject-verb inversion after a fronted adverbial of place: *Under the thick, green growth lurked the crocodile*.	Considering more formal adverbs for cohesion in non-fiction texts (e.g. using *specifically, especially, significantly, more importantly*) to emphasise information. (See Appendix for chart providing conjuncts used for different purposes.) Developing subject–verb inversion after fronted adverbials of place: *Over the hills, through the forests and beyond the river flew the silver dragon*.

Strand 4: Verbs

The verb is a key element in a clause or sentence because it handles most of the grammatical workload. Verbs can be varied to show tense and form. Although some simple-tense verbs are a single word, many verb forms require more than one word in the form of a verb phrase. Variation and consistency in the use of verb forms increase as pupils' writing develops.

The components of a verb phrase are the main (or lexical) verb and auxiliary verbs. Auxiliary verbs increase the information around the main verb:

- *she **has been** singing*
- *he **does** look cross*
- *it **will be** built*
- *they **could have been** stopped.*

Auxiliary verbs can be divided into two types:

- **primary auxiliaries**, which can also occur alone as main verbs (*be*, *have*, *do*).
- **modal auxiliaries**, which are used to build up verb phrases and contain an element of possibility, probability, intention, ability, obligation, etc. (*will*, *may*, *can*, *must*, *ought (to)*, *shall*, *might*, *could*, *would*, *should*). The future tense is created using the modal verbs *will* and *shall*.

The lexical meaning of the verb provides certain information, but there is much more we can glean.

The position reveals:

- who the subject/agent is
- who is being affected (object).

The tense and form reveal:

- when the action takes place, or when state of existence or ownership takes place (*He jumps the fence. She will be happy. He owned a car. The baby is crying.*)
- an element of duration or frequency (present perfect: *She has always cycled to work*; past perfect: *He had been prime minister.*)
- the speaker's or writer's feelings, including emphasis (*We ought to write to them. We must refuse. We could attend the meeting.*)
- negative action/existence (*He can't go to the ball. She is not content.*)
- clues as to sentence type (statement, question, command) indicated by word order and form of verb – for example, imperative (*Eat it.*), modal forms in questions (*Did you know about it?*)

One difficulty teachers face is that most speech and authentic texts use a mixture of verb forms and sometimes tenses. This allows subtle yet complex information to be conveyed in a natural way, but when teaching verbs it is important to consider which parts of the text to focus on to avoid confusing pupils with differing forms. Selecting carefully will provide opportunities to experiment with these examples and help pupils use them independently where appropriate.

Forms and tenses

The **simple** form:

- **present simple:** *I look, he cooks, they sing* (third person in the present simple is indicated by -*s* or -*es* suffixes: *she sings, he does*. The person is also indicated in the irregular verbs *be* and have: *I am, you are, it is, she has, we have*.) The present simple often portrays habitual actions and general truths.
- **past simple:** *I looked, he cooked, they sang* (irregular past tenses do not use the -*ed* suffix). In the present simple, the action is over and done with.

The **progressive** form indicates an action that is or was continuing. It incorporates a form of the verb *be* as an auxiliary in the present or past tense:

- **present progressive:** *I am looking, he is cooking, they are singing.*
- **past progressive:** *I was looking, he was cooking, they were singing.*

The main verb in the -*ing* form is called the *present participle*.

The **perfect** form incorporates a form of the verb *have* as an auxiliary in the present or past tense. It indicates actions that have been completed, but the effects or consequences of these actions are still relevant at the time referred to:

- **present perfect:** *I have looked, he has cooked, they have sung*. (The timescale referred to is up to the present and the possibility exists that the action can be continued.)
- **past perfect:** *I had looked, he had cooked, they had sung*.

The main verb in this -*ed* or irregular past tense form is called the *past participle*.

Modals express:

- ability (be able to or capable of): *We can/could go to the ball.*
- permission (be allowed or permitted to): *Can/may/might we go to the ball?*
- possibility (theoretical or factual): *We can/could go to the ball.*
- intention (willingness): *We shall/will/would go to the ball.*
- insistence: *We shall/will go to the ball.*
- obligation/compulsion: *We should/must/have to/ought to go to the ball.*
- prediction (specific, timeless, habitual): *We will go to the ball.*
- probability: *We would go to the ball.*
- necessity: *We need to/have to/must go to the ball.*

The passive voice

We usually write in the active voice. In this structure, the subject of the sentence is the person or thing doing the action and the object is what is being affected by the action. For example:

The dog chased the cat.
S V O

The passive voice uses a form of the verb *be* and the past participle of the main verb (see Appendix for a list of irregular past participles). In the passive voice, the person or thing being affected by the action becomes the subject of the sentence; the person or thing doing the action may or may not be provided. For example:

The cat was chased.
S V (past passive form)

The cat was chased by the dog
S V A (preposition + the agent)

The list below shows the most common variations of different tenses and verb forms in the passive, using the main verb constructed.

- *It is constructed.* (simple present passive)
- *It was constructed.* (simple past passive)
- *It is being constructed.* (present progressive passive)
- *It was being constructed.* (past progressive passive)
- *It has been constructed.* (present perfect passive)
- *It had been constructed.* (past perfect passive)
- *It will be constructed.* (simple future passive)
- *It is going to be constructed.* (simple future passive (is going to))
- *It could have been constructed.* (conditional present perfect passive)

Pupils should understand that the passive is used in more formal writing and that it is often used to distance the writer from the content being presented. In some cases this enables the writer to 'hide' responsibility. Of course, when writing, we may not know who the agent is and cannot include this information in a sentence. For example, in journalistic writing the perpetrator of a crime may not be known (*The statue was damaged last night, at around ten*). The passive may also be used if the agent is irrelevant to the text or to focus on the person or thing being affected (*Stonehenge was built thousands of years ago*).

Subjunctive

Verbs in the subjunctive mood are used to express a hypothetical situation or one in which something is demanded, recommended, hoped for or expected. It is only used in formal writing.

There are different ways of forming the subjunctive (see appendix). It is likely that teaching at Year 6 will focus on using subordinate clauses introduced by *if*, which express a hypothetical situation: *If … were …* . In these structures, the first and third person singular past form *was* is changed to *were*. (*If he were a better swimmer, he would have won the race.; If I were to leave, I would miss the final speech.*)

Although Appendix 2 of the National Curriculum does not specifically state that **present/past progressive, present perfect** and **subjunctive** forms are terminology for pupils, these terms do appear in the sample KS2 grammar, punctuation and spelling test. They are therefore included here where the form is first introduced to pupils.

	Y1	Y2	Y3/4	Y5/6
National Curriculum content: Verbs	**Suffixes** that can be added to **verbs** where no change is needed in the spelling of root words (e.g. *helping, helped, helper*). How the **prefix** *un-* changes the meaning of **verbs** and **adjectives** (negation, for example, *unkind*, or undoing: *untie the boat*).	Correct choice and consistent use of **present tense** and **past tense** throughout writing. Use of the **progressive** form of **verbs** in the **present** and **past tense** to mark actions in progress (for example, *she is drumming, he was shouting*). verb tense (past, present) present progressive past progressive **Apostrophes** to mark where letters are missing in spelling. apostrophe	Use of the **present perfect** form of **verbs** instead of the simple past (*for example, He has gone out to play* contrasted with *He went out to play*). present perfect Standard English forms for verb inflections, instead of local spoken forms (for example, *we were* instead of *we was*, or *I did* instead of *I done*).	Indicating degrees of possibility using **modal verbs** (for example, *might, should, will, must*). Use of the **passive** to affect the presentation of information in a **sentence** (for example, *I broke the window in the greenhouse* versus *The window in the greenhouse was broken (by me)*.) Converting **nouns** or **adjectives** into **verbs** using **suffixes** (for example, *-ate; -ise; -ify*). **Verb prefixes** (for example, *dis-, de-, mis-, over-* and *re-*). modal verb active passive subjunctive cohesion The difference between vocabulary typical of informal speech and vocabulary appropriate for formal speech and writing (for example, *find out – discover; ask for – request; go in – enter*). Linking ideas across paragraphs using tense choices (for example, he *had* seen her before). Recognise and use vocabulary and structures that are appropriate for formal speech and writing, including the **subjunctive**.

	Y1	Y2	Y3/4	Y5/6
Preparation or consolidation	Understanding when to use present and past tenses, as part of suffix teaching. Creating oral sentences in the past and present. Recognising and using the past tense for stories. Encouraging the correct use of subject–verb agreement.	Consolidating *doing/being/having* verbs. Encouraging the correct use of subject–verb agreement and Standard English forms for verb inflections. Consolidating and developing the range of irregular verbs pupils know.	Encouraging the correct use of subject–verb agreement, particularly where these conflict in some dialects. Although teaching of modal verbs does not come until Y5, pupils will be using these in their speech and writing. In preparation, they should be encouraged to think about and discuss the differences in meaning when they use different modal verbs.	Consolidating understanding around all the studied verb forms and when it is most appropriate to use them. Take opportunities to notice and discuss these in texts being studied. (Link the teaching of modal verbs to the use of apostrophes for contractions where applicable.)
Tricky bits	Understanding which part of the sentence is the verb. Lots of talk will be needed to establish this. Using the Toolkit hammer with an action will help pupils identify the patterns in a sentence. Using the suffix *-ing* requires pupils to understand the auxiliaries of the verb *be*. Using the suffix *-ed*, pupils will sometimes try to regularise irregular verbs. These need to be corrected and explained. Refer to verbs as 'being' and 'having', as well as 'doing' words.	Teachers need to be able to identify texts with good examples of the present and past simple, and the present and past progressive. Many good texts will have a sophisticated mixture of verb forms and tenses, so examples should be chosen carefully. Teachers should also understand that the term *progressive* is the same as *continuous*, which is terminology used in some grammar texts (including the *Sentence Toolkit*). Pupils need to be able to use and understand how the verb *be* alters as auxiliary in both the present and past tenses.	Using the correct Standard English forms of the past participle where these conflict with local dialect/home use. Understanding how the verb *have* alters as an auxiliary in the present tense. Understanding past participles of the irregular verbs (see Appendix for list). Understanding how the present perfect differs in meaning to other past tense forms of the verb. This will require modelling and discussion around the meanings.	Pupils may have difficulty understanding use of the subjunctive, particularly if they are already struggling with subject–verb agreement (*was/were*).

	Y1	Y2	Y3/4	Y5/6
Going beyond		Look at how the verb *have* is formed in the present tense, with a different spelling for third person singular.	Once pupils understand the present perfect, develop the use of the past perfect, particularly where there are examples in the texts being used.	More able writers could investigate different forms of the passive voice and subjunctive mood. (See appendix for subject knowledge around these items.)

Strand 5: Cohesion

It is important to link and sequence ideas in writing, so that a text flows well and makes sense to a reader. Different language devices are used to hold a text together and signpost to the reader how different parts relate to one another. This is called 'cohesion'. Where possible and relevant, the objectives in this strand have been linked to other strands. Some cohesive objectives will need to be covered within teaching and learning sequences, as they refer to links within and between sections of the text, rather than purely to sentence construction.

In the primary National Curriculum, cohesion covers verb tense consistency, appropriate choice of pronoun to avoid repetition, adverbials and lexical cohesion, such as the use of synonyms and antonyms.

Verb tense and form

Cohesion can be established by using the same tense/form throughout a piece of writing and by selecting the correct tense – for example, when expanding verb phrases. Experienced writers move between tenses and forms in a sophisticated way for effect, but pupils often find maintaining consistency more problematic. They may start a recount in the past tense and move into the present tense later, or slip into the past tense in a set of instructions when they started in the imperative.

Pronouns

Personal and possessive pronouns can be used to avoid repetition:

- *My husband has retired. He is enjoying himself.*
- *I found a pencil case in the playground. Sophie told me it was hers.*

Relative pronouns can be used to refer to something that has already been mentioned:

- *The red car, which was being driven by the robber, screamed up the road.*
- *The politician, who was not very popular, left the venue through the back door.*

Many determiners can also act as pronouns and replace a noun:

- **demonstratives:** *this, that, these, those (King Henry had already married twice, but **that** didn't stop him marrying again. Would you like some cakes? Yes, I'll take **these** please.)*
- **universal determiners:** *each, every, all, both (I went into the shop to choose between two books and came out with **both**.)*
- **partitive determiners:** *some, someone, anyone, anybody, no one, none, neither, either (I saw a red and a blue blouse, but I didn't like **either**.)*
- **quantifiers:** *many, much, few, several (There were **many** pupils on the beach and I knew **several**.)*
- **numerals – cardinal and ordinal:** *one, the first (I have lots of friends, but she was **the first**.)*

Adverbials

Conjuncts (connecting adverbs) link sentences and paragraphs throughout a text to help a reader follow meaning (see p. 24). For example, in instructions, using conjuncts will help the reader with the sequencing of the information: *first, next, after that, finally*. In a persuasive text, readers can be assisted through the use of signalling words: *moreover, in addition, furthermore*.

It is important to consider which conjuncts (connecting adverbs) are appropriate to the text type. The conjuncts used in a story are not necessarily appropriate for an explanation or a non-chronological report.

Lexical cohesion

Lexical cohesion relies on vocabulary choice. At primary level, this involves:

- repetition of vocabulary
- synonyms or near synonyms/antonyms
- superordinates (words that include the meaning of another word, e.g. *cat* is a superordinate word for *lion*)
- words that are closely related to the item being discussed.

The following paragraph shows examples of lexical cohesion: repetition of *lion*, a synonym in the *king of animals*, *cat* as a superordinate. It also includes the word *mane*, which is closely associated with lions. *Regal* and *king* are also related.

Lions are unique in that they are the only cats to live in groups (prides). Male lions are also the only cats that have manes, giving them a regal appearance that has earned them the title 'king of the beasts'. This king of animals is a top predator.

Ellipsis

Ellipsis is the omission of words that would otherwise be repeated. It is more common in speech than in writing, but some of the examples of ellipsis below may be useful in teaching cohesion in dialogue.

Noun/pronoun ellipsis:

- In compound sentences, often the subject is omitted before the second verb (*The dog barked and jumped*).
- The noun can also be omitted by using *have*. (*She probably has a temperature – she certainly looks as if she has*).

Verbal ellipsis (usually lexical verb, although auxiliaries can be ellipted):

- *Have you been playing? Yes I have.*
- *What have you been doing? Swimming.*
- If you have just described an action or a state and you want to introduce a new, contrasting subject, use than + the auxiliary verb. (*She can see better than he can. He was earning more than I was.*)
- To change the verb tense/form or modality (*They would stop if they could. Very few of us want to go, although we know we must. The poster should have created more interest than it has.*)
- Often used in the passive (*I'm sure it was repeated on the news. It must have been.*)
- *Do* is often used (*Do the pupils want to come? I think they do. Does the parrot talk? Yes he does. No he doesn't.*)

Adjective ellipsis (when using the verb *be*):

- *I think you are right. I'm sure I am.*
- *She was great! I thought she might be.*

Clausal ellipsis:

- *He advised her to visit a doctor, but she couldn't afford to.* (infinitive verb)
- *Do you think parents know how long planning takes? No, I don't think they do.*
- *Has she got any idea about how he feels? She should (have).*
- *Will she be happy there? She'd better (be).*
- *Who was going to switch on the Christmas lights? The mayor was.*

	Y1	Y2	Y3/4	Y5/6
National Curriculum content: Cohesion	Sequencing **sentences** to form short narratives. (To be taught through teaching and learning sequences.)	Correct choice and consistent use of present tense and past tense throughout writing. (Link with teaching of verbs.) tense (past, present)	Appropriate choice of **pronoun** or **noun** within and across **sentences** to aid cohesion and avoid repetition. (Link with teaching of noun/noun phrases.) pronoun possessive pronoun Introduction to paragraphs as a way to group related material. Headings and sub-headings to aid presentation. Use of paragraphs to organise ideas around a theme. (To be taught through teaching and learning sequences.)	Devices to build **cohesion** within a paragraph (for example, *then, after that, this, firstly*) (Link with teaching of adverbials.) Linking ideas across paragraphs using **adverbials** of time (for example, *later*), place (for example, *nearby*) and number (for example, *secondly*) or tense choices (for example, he *had* seen her before). (Link with teaching of adverbials and verbs.) How words are related by meaning as synonyms and antonyms (for example, *big, large, little*). (Link with teaching of noun/noun phrases.) synonym antonym

	Y1	Y2	Y3/4	Y5/6
National Curriculum content: Cohesion (continued)				Linking ideas across paragraphs using a wider range of **cohesive devices**: repetition of a **word** or phrase, grammatical connections (for example, the use of **adverbials** such as *on the other hand*, *in contrast*, or *as a consequence*) and **ellipsis**. (Link with various strands and also to be taught in teaching and learning sequences.) Layout devices (for example, headings, sub-headings, columns, bullets, or tables, to structure text). (To be taught through teaching and learning sequences.) cohesion
Preparation or consolidation	Preparing pupils for Y2 by noticing when the past and present tenses are used in different text types. (Link with verb strand.)	Consolidating pronoun use.	Consolidating pronoun use and linking with Standard English so that the correct subject and object pronouns are used. Start considering how nouns with similar meanings can be used to vary writing (e.g. *girl*, *child*, *youngster*). The term *synonym* is not needed until Y5/6. (Link with noun/noun phrase strand.)	Consolidating work on adverbials, particularly those that refer to something that has happened earlier in the text or those that help sequence information.

	Y1	Y2	Y3/4	Y5/6
Tricky bits	Making sure pupils understand that sequencing information will help their reader understand what they want to say in a story. Noticing and developing their own range of words to help sequence stories (e.g. *the next day*, *later*, *after*). (Link with adverbial strand.) Making sure the correct pronouns are used to avoid too much repetition of nouns. (Link with noun/noun phrase strand.)	Keeping tense consistent throughout a text, particularly in stories where dialogue is used. The narrative is likely to use the past tense, but dialogue usually uses the present tense. Pupils will need help checking that they have returned to past tense in the narrative. (Link with verb strand.) Tense consistency may be difficult for some EAL pupils.	Cohesion will link with work on fronted adverbials, although most of the Y3/4 adverbial work will involve adverbials as additional information. Teachers should be clear about the function of these different types of adverbials (see 'Ways of connecting ideas' in the Appendix). Pupils will need to remember to use a comma after fronted adverbials. (Link with adverbial strand.)	Understanding the meaning of some of the conjuncts (connecting adverbs) (e.g. *furthermore*, *nevertheless*). (Link with adverbial strand.) Understanding which conjuncts (connecting adverbs) are appropriate for different text types. It will help to collect appropriate conjuncts (connecting adverbs) for each text type and discuss how they help the text to flow for the reader. (Link with adverbial strand.) Pupils may have been told not to repeat themselves, so using repetition for cohesion and effect will require good examples in texts and discussion around how these are used. Ellipsis as an alternative to repetition can be introduced when writing dialogue. Pupils should problem-solve examples to decide what information has been missed out and how the structure works.
Going beyond	Developing a range of words to help sequence non-fiction texts (e.g. instructions, recounts). (Link with adverbial strand.)		Developing adverbials for cohesion where appropriate to the text type. More able writers can start collecting a range of conjuncts (connecting adverbs) for different purposes. (Link with adverbial strand.)	More able writers can develop their use of ellipsis in dialogue. Developing wider understanding of how synonyms, antonyms and superordinates can be used to write cohesively. (Link with noun/noun phrase strand.)

Strand 6: Punctuation

Punctuation should always be taught in the context of writing for a particular purpose and audience. Where relevant, the National Curriculum punctuation requirements have been embedded in the progression charts above – for example, commas in a list when teaching pupils to add more than one adjective into a noun phrase. This will help pupils understand where and when punctuation is correct or appropriate. Other punctuation marks should be covered when the text being used exemplifies them well, so they will be linked to particular teaching and learning sequences.

Punctuation is a system of symbols and marks that help organise writing and make its meaning clear. When we speak, in addition to the words we use, our listener can use a range of cues to help make sense of what we say: expression, tone, volume, body language, etc. All of these aid meaning. This is often much more than comprehension of the words and includes the emotional content and nuances of the message. In writing, however, these signals are not available – punctuation marks are used to clarify the full meaning of a message.

Full stops

A full stop is used to mark the end of a sentence that expresses a statement. In a simple sentence, a statement consists of one clause and contains one verb or verb phrase. If a sentence contains more than one clause, it is a compound or complex sentence and will include one of the ways of joining clauses (see below), or a semi-colon or colon.

Question marks

A question mark is used at the end of a sentence that forms a direct question. If an indirect question is written – for example, in reported speech – then the sentence becomes a statement and a full stop should be used:

- *What's for breakfast?*
- *She asked what was for breakfast.*

Exclamation marks

Exclamation marks are generally used in writing to denote the emphasis or feeling (often surprise) that would be expressed in the spoken words.

Sentences that are exclamations (beginning with *What* or *How*) are usually punctuated with an exclamation mark: *How good to meet you!*; *What a great party this is!* Very often these expressions of emphasis and surprise are used in dialogue and are not always represented by full sentences (in the manner of natural speech). For this reason we often use exclamation marks with single words (sometimes called interjections) or phrases (*Awesome! Fantastic! Wow! Nice dress! Great party! What a day! Goodness me!*).

Some commands have exclamation marks (*Run!*, *Don't do that!*) This is particularly common in dialogue, or where a writer wants the reader to understand the urgency or curtness of the order. It is less common in longer imperative structures, such as instructions: *Check the consistency of the mixture after half an hour.*

In addition to dialogue, exclamation marks are often seen in narrative structures to highlight onomatopoeic words: *Pop! Bang! Crash!*

Because exclamation marks are often used to reflect normal speech, they are not generally used when writing formally.

Commas

Pupils should be able to understand three uses of commas.

Commas for listing. The examples below demonstrate the use of commas to separate lists of single words, phrases or clauses:

- *Ben was cold, tired, hungry and irritable.* (single adjectives)
- *He ran home as fast as he could, through the park, past the library and up the hill.* (adverbial phrases)
- *Jemima wanted a new doll, a board game, some pretty clothes and her very own pink bike.* (noun phrases)
- *Talking loudly, giggling hysterically and singing out of tune, they annoyed everyone on the train.* (clauses)

Commas to demarcate additional information. If this additional information is embedded in the sentence, pairs of commas (bracketing commas) are used either side of the word, phrase or clause:

Mrs Smith, who has been with us for four years, will be retiring at the end of the year.

If this embedded information is removed, the sentence will still have its grammatically correct structure:

Mrs Smith will be retiring at the end of the year.

Sometimes the additional information will be placed at the beginning or end of the sentence:

In my opinion, people should never keep wild animals as pets.
People should never keep wild animals as pets, in my opinion.

The additional information *in my opinion* can be removed in both examples and the sentence remains complete.

Commas to demarcate clauses that are integral to the sentence, rather than embedded as additional information. For example, commas should be used to demarcate the two clauses in a complex sentence: *As the guards looked the other way, Robin ran quickly across the passage*. This could be written as two separate sentences (*The guards looked the other way. Robin ran quickly across the passage.*), but if we are going to use the conjunction *as* to join them in a complex sentence, we need a comma between the clauses to demarcate. The subordinate clause *As the guards looked the other way* could not stand as a sentence on its own. Pupils should understand that a comma is required when an adverbial subordinate clause starts the sentence (as it is a fronted adverbial), but it is optional when the main clause comes first. In those cases commas should be used for clarity or to create a specific effect on the reader.

When reading we tend to pause at points when commas are inserted, but pupils should understand that commas are used for the above purposes and not that they are used for a pause.

Apostrophes

Apostrophes are used for contractions and to show possession. Contractions (where one or more letters are omitted) are usually used in informal writing, so pupils should understand that the most appropriate use is in dialogue, plays and forms of non-fiction where writing is more conversational – some recounted texts, advice in instructions, persuasive posters, etc.

The apostrophe should be placed where the letter/s are omitted – *it's (it is)*, *can't (cannot)*, *I'll (I will)*. The apostrophe avoids confusion with complete words that contain the same letters (*I'll – ill*, *she'll – shell*, *we're – were*). Although pupils will see the word and contracted to 'n' in everyday situations, they should be encouraged to use this only occasionally – for example, on an advert.

Pupils will come across apostrophes used for contractions in different types of text, from classic literature (*'twas*, *o'er*) to modern slang, (*nothin'*, *s'pose*, *'cause*, *'fraid*). As in all writing choices, it is essential to talk about the uses and where they are appropriate.

Possessive apostrophes show belonging:

- 's is added to singular nouns (*Jack's bag*, *the cat's dish*, *a year's duration*). This is usually the same for a noun that already ends in an s (*James's football*, *Chris's horse*).
- 's is usually added to irregular plurals that do not end in s (*men's coats*, *children's games*).
- If a plural noun already ends in an s, it only takes the apostrophe (*the footballers' injuries*, *the boys' books*, *both horses' saddles*).
- Pronouns do not need apostrophes (*The dog lost its ball*, *the car is ours*, *it was his loss*, *the pencil was hers*).
- Some names (proper nouns) do not pronounce an additional s in the possessive; the apostrophe comes after the final s of the name. This is often the case when adding an extra s would make the word awkward to say (*Achilles' heel*, not *Achilles's heel*). There is much debate over whether proper nouns ending in a sibilant sound (/s/ or /z/) should take 's or just the apostrophe to indicate possession. When working with pupils, it is best to consistently add 's, unless this makes the word awkward to say.

Pupils should understand that apostrophes are not used to form plurals. However, when reading, pupils may notice apostrophes used to form some numerical plurals, such as dates (*1860's*, *1970's*), which is a US publishing convention.

Speech marks

Also referred to as quotation marks or inverted commas, speech marks are used to mark the beginning and end of speech or a direct quotation. They are usually written or typed in double form, although British printing often uses single speech marks.

If the reporting clause occurs first, a comma should be inserted before the speech begins. Within inverted commas, punctuation should be used in the normal way, with final punctuation included if the character is finishing speaking: *Sarah whispered, 'Do you know where you are going?'*; *'Do you know where you are going?' Sarah whispered*.

If the reporting clause is embedded, a comma is used after the first part of speech and a full stop after the reporting clause. The second part of the speech then continues within speech marks: *'I will go first,' said Jim. 'Then you can follow.'*

In a direct quotation, only the punctuation used in the quotation should be copied. Quotation marks can also be used to identify a particular word or phrase in the text that you are referring to: *The term 'noun' refers to a person, an object or a place*. Enclosing a word in quotation marks can also indicate disapproval or sarcasm: *The minister has suggested more CCTV cameras for our 'protection'*.

Brackets

Often called parentheses or round brackets, these are used in a similar way to commas demarcating additional information. Bracketing commas are usually used where there is little interference with the flow of the sentence, brackets can be used for either weak or strong interruption to the flow of text:

- *William Smith (aged 39) won the marathon in record time.*
- *Swedish smörgåsbord (a selection of open sandwiches) is served each day at 1300 hours.*

Brackets are always used in pairs, so the final bracket is included even if the additional information is at the end of the sentence. A complete sentence can be written inside brackets, in which case the full stop is placed inside the final bracket: *(You may not have been aware of this.)*

Brackets are useful for providing additional comment to the reader, not directly connected to the content of the text – for example: *From next term (as you may already be aware) assemblies will take place at the end of the day, rather than the beginning.*

It is important for pupils to understand that brackets should not be overused because they can make the text seem disjointed.

Dashes

Dashes demarcate additional information in the same way as commas and brackets, but they are used for separating information that interferes with the flow of the sentence: *Using metal snares – a barbaric practice – should be banned to prevent further suffering of animals.*

As with commas, if the added information occurs at the end of the sentence, only one dash is used: *Basking sharks have huge jaws, but are actually harmless filter feeders – even though they look similar to a great white shark.*

A dash can also be used when a sentence is suddenly broken off in dialogue: *'Keep on the pavement!' shouted Mum. 'Watch out for that lo–'*. This contrasts with ellipsis use, where speech tails off more gradually.

As with brackets, overuse of dashes should be discouraged.

Hyphens

Hyphens can be used for the following purposes:

- Splitting words that do not fit at the end of a line. Pupils should be encouraged to avoid this as much as possible, but if it is necessary they should think carefully about where the hyphen should be placed. The word should be split as equally as possible, so that there is not a very small part of it on either line, and syllable boundaries should be considered as suitable break points.
- Writing double-barrelled names: *Marie-Claire, Felicity Fenton-Smythe.*
- Writing numbers in full: *fifty-four, four-ninths.*

- In compound words. Would you write *harbour-master*, *harbour master* or *harbourmaster?* Many dictionaries list the last two (without hyphens), although the hyphenated spelling can be seen in print. The rule really is to think about how clear the word is to read and understand, and to follow conventional spelling rules. If pupils are in doubt, encourage them to check in a recent dictionary.
- In compound constructions used to modify/describe nouns. English is an extremely versatile language that enables us to combine words to create effect. Pupils can be encouraged to combine words to develop description, but it is important to consider the sense of the words when combining them this way to make things clear for the reader:
  - *The dragon had shiny scales.*
  - *It was a shiny-scaled dragon.*
  - *The dragon unfolded its jade veined wings.*
  - *The dragon unfolded its jade-veined wings.*
  - *He was a late night waiter.*
  - *He was a late-night waiter.*
- In some prefixed words. Hyphens should only be used if the meaning of the word is unclear without it, or if it makes it easier to read. For example, *co-pilot* and *pre-existing* are the correct versions (copilot and preexisting being difficult to read), but *cohesive* and *preheat* do not use hyphens. Some words can be written with or without a hyphen (e.g. *co-ordinate/coordinate*). This also reflects the more frequent use of the hyphen in British English, but recognises the increase in influence of American English, where hyphens are not used as much. There are some prefixes that usually use a hyphen (*anti-, pro-, self, non-, all-*). All prefixes have a hyphen if they are followed by a proper noun (*The British are often accused of being anti-French*).

Ellipsis

The ellipsis is sometimes referred to as an *omission mark* and signifies that the writer has left a sentence incomplete and that information has been deliberately omitted. This device is often used in narrative and enables the reader to draw on their understanding of the text so far – and their knowledge of the world – to infer the consequences for character or plot. It can be used in other text types, such as journalistic writing, to represent an unfinished comment being quoted, but is rarely used in formal writing.

An ellipsis can also be used to denote words, phrases or sentences omitted from a quotation. This can be useful when a passage to be quoted is long or contains information that is not necessary for the purpose of the quote. However, care should be taken that omission of any part of the quote does not alter the original sense or distort meaning.

Semi-colons

This punctuation mark is very much a matter of authorial choice, since other options are possible when considering the way that closely related information can be written using one or two sentences.

A semi-colon can be used to join two full, closely related sentences, instead of using a conjunction or another construction that would create a complex sentence:
Men compete in the decathlon; women compete in the heptathlon.

More than two sentences can be joined with semi-colons, creating a list of closely related sentences: *Nouns denote people, objects and places; verbs denote actions or states of being; adjectives describe nouns.*

Sometimes the second sentence will begin with a connecting adverb (see adverbials on p. 34), which should not be confused with a conjunction: *Many dogs like chocolate treats; however these are not good for their health.*

A semi-colon should be able to be replaced by a full stop, which means that there should be an independent, or main clause either side of the semi-colon.

Semi-colons can also be used for a complicated list containing many items, especially if commas have already been used: *Speakers at the education conference will be Mrs Elizabeth Smith, Professor of English at Marsh University; Dr Chris Candle, Lecturer at Hyde College; Mr Adrian Poster, MSc, Adviser to the DfE; and Mrs Freda Fenton, Member of Parliament for East Drewshire.*

Colons

A colon introduces an explanation or expansion of a statement. It is always written immediately after the statement, with no space, and is never used with a dash or hyphen. A single space should be used before the text continues, unless bullet points or numbers are used on the next line to start a list. Although there is usually a full clause before the colon, the text following the colon need not be an independent clause:

- *If we continue to churn out carbon dioxide into the environment, we will experience problems in the future: climate extremes on a huge scale.* (adds explanation of the problems)
- *He had learnt two important lessons during the game: not to dive without being fouled and not to argue with the ref.* (elaborates what he had learnt)
- *There are many places I would like to visit in Italy: Rome, Florence, Venice, Sienna and Naples.* (expands the information and is also an example of a colon introducing a list)
- *Rome, Florence, Venice, Sienna and Naples: these are some of the places I would like to visit in Italy.* (the expansion is reversed and appears first – this could be introduced to more able writers to enable them to vary sentence constructions, but they should be aware that it should not be overused).

In addition to the above formats, colons are used to introduce bullet-point lists. Pupils' non-fiction texts will provide many examples of these. They will also see colons used in play scripts, as a convention for introducing the dialogue a character is to deliver.

Often people are confused about when to use a semi-colon and when to use a colon. To decide which is correct, look to see whether the second sentence explains or elaborates on the first, since in this case a colon should be used. It should also be decided that the two sentences are closely related enough that a full stop would not be the best choice. The differences can be seen in the following examples:

- *Dad was worried; the children were crying.* (The semi-colon is showing that the sentences are closely related and the suggestion is that whatever is worrying Dad is making the pupils cry)
- *Dad was worried: the pupils were crying.* (Here the colon introduces the explanation that Dad was worried because the pupils were crying.)

Bullet points/numbers

A series of bullet points or numbers will enable pupils to attach lists of information. This way of sequencing and laying details out clearly aids the reader in locating information more quickly than if it were written in large paragraphs. Lists are often introduced by some text followed by a colon. The punctuation progression chart shows the National Curriculum requirements and consolidation for each punctuation mark.

	Y1	Y2	Y3/4	Y5/6
Spaces	Separation of words with spaces.			
Sentence demarcation	Introduction to capital letters, full stops, question marks and exclamation marks to demarcate **sentences**. Capital letters for names and for the personal **pronoun**. (Link with teaching of sentence types.) letter capital letter punctuation full stop question mark exclamation mark	Use of capital letters, full stops, question marks and exclamation marks to demarcate **sentences**. (Link with teaching of sentence types.)	Continue encouraging demarcation of sentences accurately throughout, using capital letters, full stops, question marks and exclamation marks.	Punctuating simple, compound and complex sentences accurately.
Commas		Commas to separate items in a list. (Link with teaching of noun/noun phrases.) comma	Use of commas after **fronted adverbials**. (Link with teaching of adverbials) Continue teaching of using commas to separate items in a list and extend this to work on lists of adverbials.	Brackets, dashes or commas to indicate parenthesis. Use of commas to clarify meaning or avoid ambiguity. (Link with teaching of various strands.) parenthesis bracket dash ambiguity Continue teaching of using commas to separate items in a list and extend this to work on lists of adverbials and clauses.

	Y1	Y2	Y3/4	Y5/6
Apostrophes for contraction	Separation of words with spaces.	**Apostrophes** to mark where letters are missing in spelling. (Link with teaching of verbs.) apostrophe	Consolidate use of apostrophes for contraction.	Consolidate use of apostrophes for contraction (this will link well with work on modal verbs, especially when writing dialogue). Opportunities linked to work on question tags.
Apostrophes for possession		Apostrophes to mark singular possession in nouns (for example, *the girl's name*). (Link with teaching of noun/noun phrases) apostrophe	**Apostrophes** to mark singular and **plural** possession (for example, *the girl's name, the girls' names*). (Link with teaching of noun/noun phrases.)	Consolidate use of apostrophes for possession.
Speech			Introduction to inverted commas to **punctuate** direct speech. Use of inverted commas and other **punctuation** to indicate direct speech (for example, a comma after the reporting clause; end punctuation within inverted commas: *The conductor shouted, 'Sit down!'*) (Link with teaching of sentence types.) direct speech speech marks	Consolidate using speech punctuation and layout correctly.

Other punctuation is covered in Years 5 and 6, as follows:

	Y5/6
Other punctuation	Layout devices (for example, headings, sub-headings, columns, bullets or tables, to structure text). (To be taught through teaching and learning sequences) bullet point Use of the semi-colon, colon and dash to mark the boundary between independent **clauses** (for example, *It's raining; I'm fed up*). (Link with teaching of co-ordination and subordination.) semi-colon colon dash Use of the colon to introduce a list and use of semi-colons within lists. (To be taught through teaching and learning sequences.) colon semi-colon **Punctuation** of bullet points to list information. (To be taught through teaching and learning sequences.) bullet point How hyphens can be used to avoid ambiguity (for example, *man eating shark* versus *man-eating shark*, *or recover versus re-cover*). (Link with teaching of noun/noun phrases.) hyphen

Teaching activities

Strand 1: Different ways to construct sentences

Y1	**Strand 1a: Simple sentences**
National Curriculum content: • How **words** combine to make **sentences**. • Introduction to capital letters, full stops … to demarcate **sentences**. • Capital letters for names and for the personal **pronoun**. • Sequencing **sentences** to form short narratives.	Terminology for pupils: *word* *sentence* *letter* *capital letter* *punctuation* *full stop*

Pupils need to:

- orally rehearse sentences
- understand that we write in units of meaning called sentences
- understand that a sentence contains information about someone or something that *does*, *is* or *has* something; it may include *where*, *when* or *how* this happens
- ask and answer questions about the information in a sentence
- talk about the sentences they have written and explain why they are sentences
- recognise a full stop
- understand that a written sentence starts with a capital letter and ends with a full stop
- punctuate either orally or with an action.

Activity 1a.1: What's in a picture? Resources: *Playing with Friends* PDF	Terminology for pupils: *sentence* *word*

The purpose of this activity is to:

- orally rehearse sentences
- understand that we write in units of meaning called sentences
- understand that a sentence contains information about someone or something that *does*, *is* or *has* something; it may include *where*, *when* or *how* this happens
- ask and answer questions about the information in a sentence
- talk about the sentences they have written and explain why they are sentences.

Teach

Choose a picture from the resource provided or another text. Model generating simple sentences based on what you can see. For example, using p. 15 of *Playing with Friends*: 'The boy is roller skating.'

Model asking questions to expose the grammatical structure of the sentence:

- Who is roller skating? (subject)
- What is the boy doing? (verb)

Then try the same thing with sentences containing an object. For example, using p. 17: 'The boy is riding the horse.'

- Who is riding the horse? (subject)
- What is the boy doing? (verb)
- What is the boy riding? (object)

All answers should be given in full sentences. Pupils should know when they have used a full sentence. They should be able to explain that in a full sentence there is someone (subject) who is doing something (verb) as a minimum. Some sentences will also include the person or thing that the verb is acting on (object).

Practise
Put pupils in pairs with different pictures from the resource. They should take it in turns to ask and answer questions in full sentences.

This could be developed into a game of bingo using cards made of pictures from the resource. One pupil asks a question and others see if they have the picture on their card to answer the question. The pupil who answers asks the next question. This could be played as a whole class, in small groups or in pairs.

Apply
Pupils choose some of the pictures and write sentences to go with them. In pairs, they check each other's writing to see if they have used full sentences.

Activity 1a.2: Hammer those verbs! Resources: the hammer from the *Sentence Toolkit* and a toy hammer, *A Dog's Day* PDF, photographs of people doing things (p. 81)	Terminology for pupils: *sentence* *word*

The purpose of this activity is to:

- understand that a sentence contains information about someone or something that *does*, *is* or *has* something; it may include *where*, *when* or *how* this happens.

Pupils do not need to use the terminology *verb*, *subject* and *object*, but it may be useful to start exposing them to this vocabulary.

Teach
Revisit the oral and written sentences from the previous session. Introduce the practice of 'hammering' your hand with your fist or with the toy hammer every time you hear what a person is *doing*, *being* or *having*. Once pupils have understood this concept with one sentence, they should start to do the same with a sequence of sentences. You could choose these from any book you are working on in class, or you could adapt these from *A Dog's Day*. For example: 'Rosie woke up. She came down stairs. She noticed something terrible. Rosie ran outside. The butcher pointed down the street. The shoe shop was a mess. Rosie yelled with excitement.'

Practise
Show the pupils the selection of photographs provided, or use your own. In pairs, pupils should generate sentences to go with the images. Get pupils to share some of their sentences, and the rest of the group can try to hammer when they hear the verb.

Apply
Write the sentences that the pupils have generated and underline the 'hammer' words (verbs). Create a display of these words that includes the single verbs and verb phrases (e.g. *was swimming*, *was playing*, *played*).

Activity 1a.3: Stop! Resources: screwdriver from the *Sentence Toolkit*, *Eleanor Won't Share* PDF	Terminology for pupils: *punctuation* *full stop* *capital letter*

The purpose of this activity is to:

- recognise a full stop
- understand that a written sentence starts with a capital letter and ends with a full stop
- punctuate either orally or with an action
- write a sequence of sentences in fiction or information.

Teach
Use a fiction book from your teaching sequence or the resource *Eleanor Won't Share*. Read the whole story. Choose pictures and ask pupils to generate sentences orally that are linked to the picture. Model marking the end of a sentence with the screwdriver and an appropriate action to represent the full stop.

As a class, talk about how sentences need capital letters. Make up your own symbol and action for a capital letter.

Practise
In pairs, pupils should use another two images to create sentences orally, using the actions for punctuation. When pupils are learning and remembering texts as part of the teaching sequence, ensure that they include actions for punctuation.

Apply
Pupils should write a sequence of sentences with the correct use of capital letters and full stops. The sentences could be based on images used previously or in cross-curricular activities.

Activity 1a.4: Silly sentences Resources: subject/object, verb and adjective cards (pages 81–82), hammer and screwdriver from the *Sentence Toolkit*	Terminology for pupils: *sentence* *word* *punctuation* *full stop*

The purpose of this activity is to practise forming sentences using different grammatical elements. Sentences must have at least a subject and verb.

Teach
Model creating silly sentences with the cards by choosing one card from the first pile and the verb pile. Who can make the silliest sentence that is grammatically accurate? Help pupils assess their own work by getting them to ask questions:

- Does this make a sentence? Do you need another card to make a complete sentence?
- Does your verb agree with the subject? (Use the hammer to check where the verb comes in the sentence)
- How would you punctuate your sentence? (Use the screwdriver to reinforce the punctuation.)

Practise
After creating their sentences, pupils could act it out and then write it. See if they can write the sentence that comes after this one.

Activity 1a.5: Sort it! Resources: sentence cards (p. 83)	Terminology for pupils: *sentence*

The purpose of this activity is to assess whether pupils can identify what makes a sentence.

As a group, pupils sort the cards into two sets – those that make sentences and those that don't. Look at the cards in the two groups and ask pupils to explain their decisions. Use what they say to assess understanding about sentences. Identify the elements that need further teaching.

Y1	**Strand 1b: Co-ordination and subordination**

National Curriculum content: • Joining words and joining clauses using *and*. • Introduction to capital letters, full stops … to demarcate sentences.	Terminology for pupils: *sentence* *capital letter* *punctuation* *full stop*

Pupils need to:

- understand that we can use *and* to add two words together in a sentence, when those two things are acting or being affected in the same way (e.g. *Jack and Jill went up the hill*. Both Jack and Jill are acting in the same way. *Fred was tired and hungry*.)
- understand that we can join two sentences together using the word *and*; when this happens we will only need one full stop at the end
- understand that *and* means we are adding information
- understand that, although these structures occur in a 'stream' in speech, it is important not to use too many clauses in one sentence
- orally rehearse sentences
- punctuate either orally or with an action.

Activity 1b.1: Likes/dislikes Resources: like/dislike cards (p. 84)	Terminology for pupils: *sentence*

The purpose of this activity is to:

- understand that we can use *and* to add two words together in a sentence, when those two things are acting or being affected in the same way (e.g. *Jack and Jill went up the hill*. Both Jack and Jill are acting in the same way. *Fred was tired and hungry*.)
- understand that *and* means we are adding information.

Teach
Write the word *and* on the board and ask pupils to give you an example of how they might use it. Discuss with them what it means and what job it does. You could create a symbol to represent the meaning (perhaps an addition sign).

Model using *and* to use more than one subject or object in a sentence. Use the list of things pupils might like or dislike. Choose a statement and ask who likes/dislikes this. Model creating a sentence with two or more people in the subject position – for example, *Liz and Harry like chocolate*.

Practise
In pairs or groups, pupils should use the statement cards (or ones you have created) to build sentences using *and* to link subjects or objects.

Apply
Pupils should try writing sentences linking two nouns with *and* using different verbs.

Activity 1b.2: Physical sentences Resources: *and* cards (p. 84), sentences from *All About Flowers* on cards (pages 85–86), glue gun from the *Sentence Toolkit*, pieces of wood/dowel	Terminology for pupils: *sentence*

The purpose of this activity is to:

- understand that we can join two sentences together using the word *and*; when this happens we will only need one full stop at the end
- understand that *and* means we are adding information
- understand that, although these structures occur in a 'stream' in speech, it is important not to use too many clauses in one sentence.

Teach
Use the sentences from *All About Flowers* to model how it can get boring if you write lots of short sentences that are very similar. Model joining two of the sentences, with pupils coming up to the front of the class holding cards with the sentences on, while another pupil, holding the *and* card 'stuck' in between them with the glue gun: *Some flowers look like a star* ***and*** *some flowers look like a bell*.

Discuss where the full stop needs to go in the new sentence (physically have a pupil holding a full stop on a card). Emphasise that we have made two sentences into one sentence using *and*.

Model hammering the verbs in the new sentence. Some sentences have more than one verb.

Teaching points:

- The conjunction *and* is simply sticking two sentences (clauses) together.
- Often you can remove the repeated subject: *Some flowers look like a star and some look like a bell*.

Model the danger of overusing *and*. Use pieces of dowel and sticky putty to represent clauses and the glue from the glue gun. Use sticky putty to join two pieces of dowel (they should stick together). Two clauses can be joined in this way, with the 'glue' linking the clauses to make a sentence. If you try to add a third piece of dowel, the structure will be weaker and may bend. Pupils should see that it is best to only join two (maximum three) clauses before using a full stop. You can model sticking more bits of dowel on so that the whole 'sentence' falls apart. If not using the *Sentence Toolkit*, pupils can use their hands as the 'glue' to stick clauses together. They will be able to hold two clause cards in one hand to make a sentence, then add another clause card while still holding the second and third clauses – but after that they will run out of hands!

Discuss how a sentence that has lots of *ands* is boring and difficult to read.

Practise
In pairs, pupils should use more sentences from *All About Flowers* (or a different text) to try joining some of the sentences with *and*. Share these sentences with the class or another group and discuss:

- if they make sense and why they chose the sentences to join
- if they are punctuated correctly
- if they communicate the information more clearly.

Apply
Pupils should either write their own version of the book *All About Flowers* or create a similar piece of information writing about a subject they are familiar with. Decide when to use *and* to join words or clauses. Punctuate compound sentences with full stops and capital letters.

Activity 1b.3: What's in a picture? Resources: *and* cards, a picture with a lot of activity taking place (e.g. the PDF picture of a Roman fort from pages 26–27 of *Life in Roman Britain*), glue gun and screwdriver from the *Sentence Toolkit*	Terminology for pupils: *sentence* *full stop* *punctuation*

The purpose of this activity is to:

- understand that we can join two sentences together using the word *and*; when this happens we will only need one full stop at the end
- understand that *and* means we are adding information
- understand that, although these structures occur in a 'stream' in speech, it is important not to use too many clauses in one sentence
- orally rehearse sentences
- punctuate either orally or with an action.

Teach
Use the picture to model orally creating sentences where more than one thing is happening, using the conjunction *and*. For example: *The servants are carrying wood and fetching water.* Use the action for the glue gun to emphasise the conjunction. Use the screwdriver action for punctuation.

Create sentences where *and* is used to join words. For example: *The soldier is wearing a helmet and a scarf*. Hammer the verbs to emphasise that pupils have joined two sentences or two words.

Practise
In pairs, pupils should choose a different picture from a relevant text in class and repeat the activity. They should report back to the class and sort their choices into sentences that use *and* to join clauses and those that use *and* to join words.

Apply
Pupils should write a short description of a picture using *and* to join words and clauses.

Y2	Strand 1b: Co-ordination and subordination
National Curriculum content: • **Subordination** (using *when*, *if*, *that*, *because*) and **co-ordination** (using *or*, *and*, *but*). • Use of capital letters, full stops … to demarcate **sentences**.	Terminology for pupils: *compound* *verb*

Pupils need to:

- understand that we can join two sentences together using the words *and*, *or*, *but*; when this happens, we have constructed one sentence with two clauses (a compound sentence)
- understand the meaning of these conjunctions: *and* = addition, *but* = contrast, *or* = alternative
- understand that when a subject is repeated, it can either be replaced with a pronoun or omitted: *George loves chocolate but (he) hates ice cream*.
- extend sentences using subordinating conjunctions such as *when*, *if*, *that*, *because* and be able to talk about how they affect the meaning of the sentence
- understand that *when*, *if*, *because* (and others) can start sentences.

Activity 1b.4: Physical sentences Resources: glue gun from the *Sentence Toolkit*, sentences to join, conjunction cards *and*, *but*, *or*, Red Riding Hood sentences (p. 87)	Terminology for pupils: *compound*

The purpose of this activity is to:

- understand that we can join two sentences together using the words *and*, *or*, *but*; when this happens, we have constructed one sentence with two clauses (a compound sentence)
- understand the meaning of these conjunctions: and = addition, but = contrast, or = alternative
- understand that when a subject is repeated, it can either be replaced with a pronoun or omitted: *George loves chocolate but (he) hates ice cream.*

Teach

Pupils have already learnt to combine words and phrases using *and*. Here we need to extend this idea to other conjunctions: *but* and *or*. Using the first four sentences for this activity in the resources, model combining sentences using *but*, *and*, *or*. Use the glue gun to illustrate that you are sticking two sentences together to make another one. Discuss how the conjunctions change the meaning. Draw out from discussion the different functions:

- *and* = addition
- *but* = opposition
- *or* = alternative

Draw attention to the fact that we can replace a repeated subject with a pronoun or omit it altogether: *The boy skated down the hill and looked worried/he looked worried.*

Get pupils to 'hammer' out the verbs to reinforce that they have now made a sentence with two verbs.

Practise

In pairs, pupils should use the Red Riding Hood sentences and the conjunctions *and*, *but*, *or* to write a short character profile. Try out different ways of joining the sentences and agree what works best and why. Share these with the class and discuss how the use of conjunctions changes the meaning.

Apply

Pupils could write a character profile of another well-known character, joining sentences with *and*, *but*, *or*. They could also find examples in texts of where these conjunctions are used well.

Activity 1b.5 Subordinating with physical sentences Resources: conjunction spanner and screwdriver from the *Sentence Toolkit*, clause examples from *Meerkats Are Awesome* (p. 87), conjunction cards, subordinate clause examples (p. 88)	Terminology for pupils: *compound* *verb*

The purpose of this activity is to:

- extend sentences using subordinating conjunctions such as *when*, *if*, *that*, *because* and be able to talk about how they affect the meaning of the sentence
- understand that *when*, *if*, *because* (and others) can start sentences.

Teach

Pupils have already learnt that two sentences can be combined by 'sticking' them together with simple conjunctions. Now they are going to learn about a different way of extending sentences and joining parts of a sentence that enables us to express more complex links between clauses.

Model joining two clauses with a subordinating conjunction. You can use the *Meerkats Are Awesome* resource, or any text written mainly in simple sentences.

Pupils hold up the two simple sentences. Ask them to talk about how these two sentences are linked in terms of meaning. Choose a conjunction and model how the conjunction makes that link. Model attaching it to one of the clauses with the spanner (fix with sticky putty).
For example:

- *They get wet and cold*. (The link here is causal so we could use *if*. *If* has to be attached to *They get wet and cold* to clarify the meaning.)
- *Pups can die*.

Model how we can also swap the clauses around once the conjunction has been fixed to a clause:

- *If they get wet and cold, pups can die.*
- *Pups can die if they get wet and cold.*

'Hammer' the verbs to show that they have made a sentence with two verbs.

Use punctuation cards and the screwdriver tools to show how to punctuate the sentence. Only use a comma to mark the clause boundary when the sentence begins with the subordinate clause (the one starting with the conjunction in this case).

With the sentences created above, ask pupils which part of the whole sentence could be a sentence on its own? Why? Explore the fact that the clause with the conjunction (the subordinate clause) needs something else in order to make sense, whereas the other part (the main clause) could be a sentence. Use the subordinate clause examples to orally complete the sentences.

As a class, look at the other pairs of sentences about meerkats. Which conjunction card could you use? Create the sentences with pupils using the cards, including punctuation.

For additional teaching, model how complex sentences can be created by starting with a conjunction.

Practise

In pairs, pupils should use the conjunction cards to create some complex sentences. You could give them your own sentences linked to cross-curricular learning or take a text and rewrite the sentences in simple form. Check that the sentences pupils come up with:

- make sense
- have at least two verbs
- are punctuated correctly
- use the conjunction at the start and sometimes in the middle.

Get pupils to explain to another pair why they have joined sentences in the way they have.

In cross-curricular contexts, set pupils challenges to orally create sentences starting with/ including the conjunctions they have learnt. For example: *Tell me about what you have learnt in your electricity investigation. Explain what you have learnt in this maths problem.*

Apply
Use examples of pupils' writing from literacy and across the curriculum to explore how sentences are linked using *and, but, or* and *when, if, because*. Avoid using *that* for this activity (see Activity 1b.6). Model combining sentences to:

- avoid repetition
- communicate meaning succinctly
- explain links between ideas
- vary the pace of writing
- avoid over-use of combining.

After modelling, get pupils to give feedback to each other about how sentences have been constructed – where it works well and where it could be improved.

Collect examples of where complex and compound sentences are used from texts and particularly pupils' own writing, and display them.

Activity 1b.6 Using *that* Resources: *Amphibians* PDF and sentence examples, *that* card and sorting chart (p. 88), conjunction spanner from the *Sentence Toolkit*	Terminology for pupils: *verb*

The purpose of this activity is to:

- extend sentences using subordinating conjunctions such as *when, if, that, because* and be able to talk about how they affect the meaning of the sentence.

Teach
The word *that* can be used as a conjunction, but it acts differently to *if, because* and *when* because the clauses cannot be swapped around.

Use the caption from p. 9 of *Amphibians* to model how two sentences have been joined by *that* (use the conjunction spanner). What is the link between the two clauses in terms of meaning? 'Hammer' out the verbs and reinforce that fact that there are two verbs because we have joined two sentences/clauses.

Practise
Pupils should use the pattern of the *Amphibians* sentence to create some of their own sentences. These can be about anything they like. For example: *I am so hungry that I could eat a horse*. Share examples and check that sentences have two verbs, make sense and are punctuated correctly.

Apply
In pairs or small groups, pupils should use the whole of the *Amphibians* book to find examples of sentences joined with *and, but, or* and sentences joined with *because, if, when, that*. Sort them on a chart based on the example in the Resources section.

Y1	Strand 1c: Sentence types

National Curriculum content:

- Introduction to capital letters, full stops, question marks and exclamation marks to demarcate **sentences**.
- Capital letters for names and for the personal **pronoun**.

Terminology for pupils:
letter
capital letter
punctuation
full stop
question mark
exclamation mark

Pupils need to:

- understand that there are different types of sentences, which have different end punctuation.

Activity: 1c.1 Playing with sentence types
Resources: images from *Goldiclucks and the Three Bears* PDF, screwdrivers for basic punctuation from the *Sentence Toolkit*

Terminology for pupils:
punctuation

The purpose of this activity is to:

- understand that there are different types of sentences, which have different end punctuation.

Teach
Use the images from *Goldiclucks and the Three Bears*. Tell the story with pupils. As you read, choose examples of where pupils could generate a question, an exclamation or a command. For example, on p. 5 pupils could ask what the little bear might be saying to his mother ('Can we go to the waterfall?', 'Hurry up!', 'What a lovely day!').

Talk to pupils about what sort of sentences these are. What do they do? Introduce the idea that we need a screwdriver to mark the end of the sentence but it is not always a full stop.

Practise/Apply
Pupils should use role-play to take different stories told through pictures (or puppets) and practise using different sentence types. Use the screwdriver if possible when orally rehearsing.

Y2	Strand 1c: Sentence types

National Curriculum content:

- How the grammatical patterns in a sentence indicate its function as a **statement, question, exclamation** or **command**.
- Use of capital letters, full stops, question marks and exclamation marks to demarcate **sentences**.

Terminology for pupils:
statement
question
exclamation
command

Pupils need to:

- understand that there are different ways of forming a sentence (questions, statements, exclamations, commands) and be able to talk about what makes them different
- understand that questions can be constructed in different ways
- be able to tell the difference between questions and exclamations beginning with *what* and *how*
- understand how to punctuate different sentence types.

Activity 1c.2 Sort it! Resources: examples of different sentence types from classroom books	Terminology for pupils: *statement* *question* *exclamation* *command*

The purpose of this activity is to:

- understand that there are different ways of forming a sentence (questions, statements, exclamations, commands) and be able to talk about what makes them different.

Teach
On the whiteboard or on cards, share different examples of sentence types that you have found in texts from the classroom. Work with pupils to:

- discuss what they notice about the sentences
- decide what is the same and what is different
- explore whether they are all sentences and how we know
- decide how they could be sorted.

Let pupils define the sorting groups, but once they have been agreed, introduce the terminology *questions*, *statements*, *exclamations* and *commands*.

Practise
Find other examples of sentences from texts that pupils can read and sort.

Activity 1c.3: Fill in the slots Resources: examples of sentence elements with additional rows to be added by pupils (p. 89)	Terminology for pupils: *statement* *question* *exclamation* *command*

The purpose of this activity is to:

- understand that there are different ways of forming a sentence (statements) and be able to talk about what makes them different
- understand how to punctuate different sentence types.

Teach
The next sequence of lessons will explore each sentence type individually. Start with statements, as these follow the most basic sentence structure.

- Recap what pupils know about statements by generating some examples. Use the examples in the Resources section to introduce the idea of the main slots in a sentence (subject, verb, object/complement).
- Help pupils fill some more slots in the table with their own ideas.
- Talk about the order of the items in the statement/sentence.
- Use the screwdriver to demonstrate use of the full stop.

Practise
In pairs, pupils should generate other sentences and write the SVO/C on different coloured cards.

Apply
Pupils should swap their cards with another pair, but muddle them up. Can they create sentences that follow the statement structure and make sense?

Activity 1c.4: Question it Resources: question word cards and question marks on cards (p. 89), question mark screwdriver from the *Sentence Toolkit*, *Meerkats Are Awesome* PDF	Terminology for pupils: *question*

The purpose of this activity is to:

- understand that there are different ways of forming a sentence (questions) and be able to talk about what makes them different
- understand how to punctuate different sentence types.

Teach
Revisit what pupils noticed about questions when they were sorting different sentence types. Model generating questions using question words and questions starting with verbs (e.g. *Can you…*).

Agree an action for the question mark screwdriver with the class. Orally create more sentences and add the question mark action at the end.

Practise
Go back to the statements written for Activity 1c.3. Can pupils turn these into questions and write them down? For example: *Meerkats dig burrows. Do Meerkats dig burrows?*

Using *Meerkats Are Awesome* or another text you are using in class, read a simple page together. In pairs, pupils should take a piece of information from the page and write a question that links to it. For example: *Up to 30 meerkats live in a mob. How many meerkats live in a mob?*

Apply
In pairs, pupils should take a different page of the book and write as many questions as they can based on the information on that page. They should try to use as many different ways of forming questions as possible. Use the question word cards for support. Make sure questions are punctuated with a question mark.

Afterwards, they should swap pages and questions with another pair. Can they answer the questions in statements using the information on the page?

Activity 1c.5: Do as I tell you Resources: 'Mini Magic Fire Extinguisher' from p. 13 of *Super Cool Chemical Reactions* PDF, full stop screwdriver from the *Sentence Toolkit*	Terminology for pupils: *command*

The purpose of this activity is to:

- understand that there are different ways of forming a sentence (commands) and be able to talk about what makes them different
- understand how to punctuate different sentence types.

Teach
Recap what pupils noticed about commands in the initial activity in this sequence. Role-play in pairs: one person tells the other to do things and they have to comply. For example: *Bend down. Put your hands on your head. Turn to the right.*

Read the text together (just the plan of action). Ask pupils to 'hammer' out the verbs. They should notice that verbs come at the start of the sentence.

Discuss where you might find commands and why. Make a list and collect examples.

Activity 1c.6: How tricky this is! Resources: exclamations on card (p. 90), *Honestly Red Riding Hood Was Rotten* PDF, exclamation screwdriver from the *Sentence Toolkit*	Terminology for pupils: *exclamation*

The purpose of this activity is to:

- understand that there are different ways of forming a sentence (exclamations) and be able to talk about what makes them different
- be able to tell the difference between questions and exclamations beginning with *what* and *how*
- understand how to punctuate different sentence types.

Teach

Exclamations are difficult to teach. Grammatically speaking, formal English requires sentences that are exclamations to begin with either *what* or *how*. But in everyday informal English you will find exclamations beginning with other words. This section will focus on exclamations starting with *what* and *how*, but you will need to be prepared for pupils spotting and using other sentences using exclamation marks.

Use the examples of exclamations to discuss the two main types of exclamations and to draw attention to the exclamation mark. Practise saying these as a class with appropriate expression and adding the exclamation mark screwdriver at the end. You could take photographs of pupils saying the statements with appropriate facial expressions. These could be used to display as a visual reminder of this sentence type.

Practise

Using *Honestly Red Riding Hood Was Rotten* or the text you are using for literacy, ask pupils to generate exclamations using *how* and *what* for appropriate bits. If it is for a text, they could write them on callouts and stick them with the text.

Activity 1c.7: More exclamations Resources: exclamation screwdriver from the *Sentence Toolkit*, exclamations chart (p. 90), statement sentences from *A Dog's Day* (p. 90), *A Dog's Day* PDF	Terminology for pupils: *exclamation*

The purpose of this activity is to:

- understand that there are different ways of forming a sentence (exclamations) and be able to talk about what makes them different
- understand how to punctuate different sentence types.

Teach

Are exclamations sentences? Look at the exclamations pupils have written and discuss if they fit what we know about sentences. They won't, because there are no subjects or verbs. Model how the subject and verb can be added and are almost implied. Use the chart of how these are constructed to discuss the pattern of exclamations (revise adjectives if needed).

How strange! How strange it is!
How horrid! How horrid that is!
How difficult! How difficult this is!

Practise

Pupils should try turning statements into exclamations using the examples in the resources (all based on *A Dog's Day*).

Apply

In a guided reading session using *A Dog's Day*, help pupils find examples of exclamations. Which are grammatically correct? How do they know? Look for all the other uses of the exclamation mark. Why have these been used? What impact do they have on the reader?

Strand 2: Nouns and noun phrases

Y1	Nouns and noun phrases
National Curriculum content: • Regular **plural noun suffixes** -*s* or -*es* (for example, *dog*, *dogs*; *wish*, *wishes*), including the effects of these suffixes on the meaning of the noun. • How the **prefix** *un-* changes the meaning of **adjectives** (negation, for example, *unkind*).	Terminology for pupils: *singular* *plural*
Pupils need to: • understand what the nouns in sentences are and how to form the plurals (link to spelling teaching) • understand that nouns can be people, places or things • understand that adjectives can be added to a noun to give more detail • understand that opposites can be created by using the prefix *un-* to adjectives.	
Activity 2.1: All in a name Resources: labels for classroom objects/people/places, noun cards (p. 91)	Terminology for pupils: *singular* *plural*

The purpose of this activity is to:

- understand what the nouns in sentences are and how to form the plurals (link to spelling teaching)
- understand that nouns can be people, places or things.

Teach 1

Make a set of labels for things in the classroom, such as *pencil*, *table*, *book*. Read them with pupils and ask them to stick them on the relevant objects. Include one or two names of people and/or places if possible.

Talk to pupils about what they were labelling and establish that they are all things, people or places. Introduce the term *noun* (not statutory terminology) and explain that names of people and places must have a capital letter. Teach them the term *proper noun* (not statutory terminology) for names of people, places, days of the week, months of the year (link to spelling programme).

Teach 2

Look at plural spellings using -*s* and -*es* and link to spelling rules. What word do we often put before a noun when there is just one? (*a*/*an*). Try out different nouns with *a*/*an* and play with the sounds. For example: *a cat*/*an elephant; a banana*/*an orange*.

Practise 1

Use both sets of noun cards in the Resources section and get pupils to sort the words into objects, places and people. Ask the following questions:
Why do some of them have capital letters?
Can they sort the objects into singular and plural?

Practise 2

Play the party game 'I went to the market and I bought…,' with each pupil adding a noun in alphabetical order. For example: *I went to the market and I bought some apples, a banana, a cat…*

Apply

Find some pictures with lots of detail and talk to pupils about what objects, people and places they can see. Model writing a few labels, including plurals, then ask pupils to continue with labelling their pictures. How many things can they find to label? Ask pupils to talk about the things they have labelled and check that they are all nouns.

Activity 2.2: Grammar goggles Resources: example sentences, noun and verb word cards (p. 92), hammer and full stop screwdriver from the *Sentence Toolkit*	Terminology for pupils: *singular* *plural*

The purpose of this activity is to:

- understand what the nouns in sentences are and how to form the plurals (link to spelling teaching).

Teach
Display the example sentences. Ask pupils to put their 'grammar goggles' on to see if they can spot the nouns in the sentences. Say the sentences together, 'hammering' the verbs and fixing the full stop with the screwdriver. Look at where the nouns come in the sentence (before and after the verb in both subject and object position). Can pupils find an example of a plural noun and one that is a person or place?

Practise
Pupils should continue to identify and mark the nouns that they find. They could use different coloured highlighters for plurals and people/places.

Apply
Give pupils the word cards with nouns and verbs and ask them to make silly sentences by combining them. Where do they need capital letters and full stops? Ask them to write out their favourite sentence, including the punctuation.

Activity 2.3 Describe the object Resources: collection of classroom objects, tape measure and paintbrush from the *Sentence Toolkit*, *Zebras Are Awesome!* PDF or another text with simple noun phrases from Activities 2.1 and 2.2 (pages 91–92)	Terminology for pupils: *singular* *plural*

The purpose of this activity is to:

- understand that adjectives can be added to a noun to give more detail.

Teach
Use a collection of objects that can be found in the classroom. Choose one and ask pupils to think of as many words as they can to describe that object. Introduce the term *adjective* (not statutory terminology) and the paintbrush as a way of 'painting' in more detail or information. Model a phrase describing the object – for example, *the red balloon*. Repeat this with different objects and record different adjectives that come up. Show pupils the tape measure and explain how we are expanding the noun into a noun phrase by adding the adjective.

Practise 1
Put all the objects in a bag. One pupil feels an object and the others ask 10 questions to try and guess what the object is. Encourage pupils to use the adjectives generated in their questions (*Is it spiky?*) When the object is revealed, practise saying phrases using the appropriate adjectives and using the paintbrush and tape measure to show the expansion.

Practise 2
Play 'Who/what am I?' Use the noun cards from Activities 2.1 and 2.2, or make your own. Stick one on each pupil's back. They walk around the room and ask other pupils questions to try and find out who/what they are. They have to ask questions that will get the other person to give some descriptive information (*Am I big or small? What colour am I?*) After the game, talk to pupils about the words that helped them guess what they were. Reinforce the expanded noun phrases with the tape measure – for example, *So, you were a furry mouse!*

Apply 1
In groups, pupils should use the objects from the session above, or others, and write their own descriptive phrases, choosing the adjective that they think best describes their object.

Link this learning to texts used in literacy sequences, and support pupils with describing nouns using adjectives.

Apply 2
Use a book such as *Zebras Are Awesome!* Read the book with pupils, particularly the first chapter. Ask pupils to put on their grammar goggles to see if they can spot noun phrases with an adjective and a noun. Model a few with them and then ask them to continue reading and highlighting other examples. Talk to pupils about what they have found to reinforce the pattern of adjective + noun. Examples include:

hungry lion
tall grass
black-and-white stripes
easier prey
dazzling stripes
brown colouring
thin, close stripes
light brown shadow stripes
wide stripes
black skin
large ears

Activity 2.4: Understanding opposites Resources: adjectives and their opposites cards (p. 93), examples of opposite sentences (p. 93), paintbrush from the *Sentence Toolkit*	Terminology for pupils: *singular* *plural*

The purpose of this activity is to:

- understand that opposites can be created by using the prefix *un-* to adjectives.

Teach
Show a range of adjectives with their opposites on the board or give pupils the cards from the Resources section. Ask pupils to read them and pair them up. Why did they choose the pairs that they did? Clarify the meaning of any unknown words. Introduce *un* as a way of transforming some adjectives into their opposites using *unhappy*, *unhelpful*, *untidy*, *unkind*, *unlucky* as examples.

Practise
Read the examples of opposite sentences; discuss the adjectives and what they tell you about the nouns. Talk to pupils about changing the meaning to the opposite and generate the adjectives they could use. Pupils should then choose sentences and rewrite them using their opposite adjectives. Reinforce the paintbrush tool to support the meaning.

Y2	**Nouns and noun phrases**
National Curriculum content: • Formation of **nouns** using **suffixes** such as *-ness*, *-er* and by compounding (for example, *whiteboard*, *superman*). • Formation of **adjectives** using **suffixes** such as *-ful*, *-less*. • Use of the **suffixes** *-er*, *-est* in **adjectives**. • Expanded **noun phrases** for description and specification (for example, *the blue butterfly*, *plain flour*, *the man in the moon*). • Commas to separate items in a list. • **Apostrophes** to mark singular possession in nouns (for example, *the girl's name*).	Terminology for pupils: *noun* *noun phrase* *compound* *adjective* *suffix* *comma*

Pupils need to:

- understand that a group of words can work together to fill the noun slot in a sentence and that this is called a *noun phrase*
- understand that a noun phrase can be replaced with a pronoun
- understand how to construct a noun phrase using determiners, adjectives and nouns (e.g. *My naughty, mean sister*)
- understand how commas are used in lists of adjectives and noun phrases
- understand how adjectives can be used in different places in a sentence: before the noun (*My naughty sister*) and after the verb (*My sister is naughty*)
- understand how adding suffixes to a word can change the meaning and/or the word class (e.g. *happy – happiness, climb – climber, play – playful*) and how nouns can be formed by compounding
- understand the difference between adding an s for a plural and adding an apostrophe s for singular possession.

Activity 2.5: Revise nouns Resources: noun category chart (p. 94)	Terminology for pupils: *noun*

The purpose of this activity is to:

- understand that nouns can be people, places or things (from Y1).

Revise and practise

Ask pupils how they would define a noun. Ask them about people and places, and revise proper nouns. Play a game of 'categories'. Ask pupils to work in pairs and fill in the chart in the Resources sections (add/replace any categories you want) to list as many nouns in the different categories as they can. Give them a time limit and see who has found the most for each category. Reinforce which nouns are proper nouns and need capital letters. Link to any spelling of proper nouns that they are revising in spelling (e.g. days of the week).

Activity 2.6: Expanding nouns Resources: *Sabretooth Cats* or *Eleanor Won't Share* PDFs or other texts with good examples of noun phrases, tape measure, paintbrush and comma screwdriver from the *Sentence Toolkit*, pre-modification chart and colour-coded sentences (p. 95)	Terminology for pupils: *noun* *noun phrase* *adjective* *comma* *determiner (from Y3/4)*

The purpose of this activity is to:

- understand that a group of words can work together to fill the noun slot in a sentence and that this is called a *noun phrase*
- understand that a noun phrase can be replaced with a pronoun
- understand how to construct a noun phrase using determiners, adjectives and nouns (e.g. *My naughty, mean sister*)
- understand how commas are used in lists of adjectives.

Teach

Use a book with good examples of noun phrases, such as *Sabretooth Cats*. Look at some of the sentences – for example: 'Their strong bodies had big muscles and short tails. The cat's two long teeth were called canines. These sharp, 18-centimetre teeth could cut through tough skin.' Ask pupils what information they discover about the cats from these sentences. Collect the words and phrases that they say.

Revise from Y1 (or teach if not previously taught) the meaning of *noun* and *adjective*, including the terminology. Introduce or revise the use of the paintbrush tool for 'painting' in more information or detail.

With pupils, sort out which words in the sentences are nouns and which are adjectives. Show pupils how the sentences still make sense if you take out the adjectives, but they offer less information. Use the tape measure to illustrate expanding and contracting the phrases.

Look at the sentences with colour coding in the Resources section. Read them with pupils, 'hammering' the verbs. Teach them that before the verb we have either a single noun (e.g. cats) or a collection of words grouped around the noun (e.g. *Their strong bodies…*). This is called a *noun phrase*. Look at the words *their, the, these* as words that introduce the noun phrase (determiners) and that also give us more information about the noun. Revise *a/an* before consonants and vowels.

Practise

Use the pre-modification chart to help pupils choose determiners and adjectives to put before the noun. Model choosing more than one adjective and separating them with commas. Practise saying the phases with the action for the comma screwdriver. Adapt the chart to include words relevant to the writing that the pupils are currently doing.

Apply

Play the party game 'The vicar's cat' but change it to 'My teacher's cat'. Go around the room, with each pupil adding an adjective in alphabetical order. For example: *My teacher's cat is an adventurous cat. My teacher's cat is an adventurous and bashful cat. My teacher's cat is an adventurous, bashful and cautious cat….* Reinforce that after each adjective there is a comma except before the final *and*.

Collect new adjectives that the pupils could use in their writing.

Activity 2.7: Playing with pronouns Resources: sentence examples (p. 95), cloze text paragraph (p. 96), *Zebras Are Awesome* PDF	Terminology for pupils: *noun phrase* *pronoun*

The purpose of this activity is to:

- understand that a noun phrase can be replaced with a pronoun.

Teach
Show pupils the first example of a sentence with an expanded noun phrase from the Resources section. Identify the expanded noun phrase and name the determiner, adjectives and nouns. Show pupils how the whole noun phrase can be replaced with a pronoun.

Practise
Pupils should work through the other sentences and replace the noun phrases with pronouns. Read some of the sentences aloud and collect the pronouns that they have used to put in a display. Explain that these are called pronouns (not statutory terminology).

Try pairing up the pronouns: *I/me; he/him* (subject and object personal pronouns).

When looking at texts in literacy, or other curriculum areas, ask pupils to collect other pronouns that they come across.

Apply
Use the cloze paragraph from p. 16 of *Zebras Are Awesome!* in the Resources section or the text you are using for your teaching sequence with some of the nouns and pronouns removed. Give pupils the pronouns and ask them to put them in the correct places. Discuss their choices. Ask pupils to tell you how they knew where to put them and what helped them make their choices.

Activity 2.8: Resources: sticky notes, paintbrush, hammer and full stop screwdriver from the *Sentence Toolkit*	Terminology for pupils: *noun* *noun phrase* *adjective*

The purpose of this activity is to:

- understand how to construct a noun phrase using determiners, adjectives and nouns (e.g. *My naughty, mean sister*).

Teach
Go round the class asking each pupil to give you an adjective. Write each one on a sticky note and stick them in a column (keep the pace rapid) on the wall. Then repeat the exercise with nouns and make a second list. Model choosing an adjective and a noun to create a noun phrase – these can be as sensible or silly as you like, for example *the bushy-tailed pencil*.

Then show pupils how the noun phrase can be re-formed into a sentence: *The pencil is bushy-tailed*. Reinforce the parts of the sentence by 'hammering' the verb (*is*) and screwing in the full stop. Look at where the adjectives have gone in the second sentence (in the complement position).

Practise
Distribute the sticky notes to groups of pupils and ask them to use the words *the* and *is* to make a noun phrase, then turn it into a sentence with a full stop. Repeat with other sticky notes. Ask them to write their favourite noun phrase and sentence in their books.

Activity 2.9: All about apostrophes Resources: *Zebras Are Awesome!* PDF, *Sabretooth Cats* PDF or other texts with good examples of noun phrases, apostrophe screwdriver from the *Sentence Toolkit*, spot the mistake paragraph (p. 97)	Terminology for pupils: *apostrophe*

The purpose of this activity is to:

- understand the difference between adding an s for a plural and adding an apostrophe s for singular possession.

Teach

From one of the resource books, or a text linked to your teaching sequence, draw pupils' attention to the apostrophe to mark the singular possessive (e.g. *The* ***cat's*** *two long teeth*) and the lack of an apostrophe in the plural (e.g. *Sabretooth* ***cats*** *were about 1 metre tall*). Ask pupils:

- Who do the teeth belong to?
- How many cats are there? (in both sentences).

Discuss how we use an apostrophe s to show that something belongs to someone. Give pupils some more sentences and ask them to answer the question: *Who does it belong to?*

Link to the spelling programme where this is practised.

Practise

Play 'Spot the mistake'. Use the passage in the Resources section, or another of your choice, and ask pupils to identify and insert the apostrophes in the correct places. Then play 'Justify'. Ask them to explain to a partner why they have put an apostrophe in a certain place. They need to explain what belongs to whom.

Apply

In writing, focus on pupils using plural s and singular possessive apostrophe s correctly. Support pupils in checking and editing their writing for this one focus.

Activity 2.10: Adjective overload? Resources: *Sabretooth Cats* PDF or other texts with good examples of noun phrases, tape measure and comma and full stop screwdrivers from the *Sentence Toolkit*, pre-modification chart (p. 97), word cards based on the text from your teaching sequence	Terminology for pupils: *noun* *noun phrase* *adjective* *apostrophe* *comma*

The purpose of this activity is to:

- understand that a group of words can work together to fill the noun slot in a sentence and that this is called a *noun phrase*
- understand that a noun phrase can be replaced with a pronoun
- understand how to construct a noun phrase using determiners, adjectives and nouns (e.g. *My naughty, mean sister*)
- understand how commas are used in lists of adjectives.

Teach

Make word cards based on the text you are using in your teaching sequence. Show pupils how to use them to play 'Physical phrases' by choosing and moving the cards around, using determiners, adjectives and nouns. Practise saying the phrases with the action for the comma screwdriver.

Use the tape measure to demonstrate what happens if we put too many adjectives before the noun (it begins to go floppy and we lose the impact of the description). Look at the adjectives in the phrase and decide which ones are important to the description and which ones are not. Take out those that do not add much to the description. Then show that the whole noun phrase can be reduced to one word (e.g. *tigers* or *they* – single noun or pronoun).

Practise
Repeat the activity with pupils working in pairs, using the pre-modification chart to construct their noun phrases and record them. Encourage them to add other words that are not on the chart that they want to use. Reinforce using commas where adjectives are in a list.

Get pupils to read out their phrases. Have they put in the commas? Have they put in too many adjectives that make the tape measure go floppy? Can they reduce the phrase using just the noun or pronoun? Are there any nouns that need a possessive apostrophe?

Apply
Model using noun phrases (with one or more adjectives and different determiners) to create sentences about an animal that the pupils are going to write about. If the text model is appropriate, play 'Pattern It' to support pupils in replacing the adjectives and nouns with others generated by the class. For example, use a section from *Sabretooth Cats* to write about triceratops: *Their bodies had powerful, muscular legs and three strong horns. These sharp horns could protect them from dangerous predators.* Ask the pupils to read their sentences and to use the comma and full stop screwdrivers to fix the punctuation in the correct places.

Activity 2.11: I went to the market Resources: comma screwdriver from the *Sentence Toolkit*, example noun phrases (p. 97)	Terminology for pupils: *noun* *noun phrase* *adjective* *comma*

The purpose of this activity is to:

- understand how commas are used in lists of adjectives and noun phrases.

Revise
Play 'Be the teacher'. Write a sentence on the board with lots of adjectives but no commas, then ask the pupils to 'be the teacher' and mark the sentence by putting in the commas. Why did they need to put them in?

Teach
Show pupils the list of noun phrases with no commas from the Resources section. Can they read it easily? How would commas help with this list? Get the pupils to show you where the commas should go. Introduce the idea that commas are used to separate both words and phrases in lists.

Practise
Play 'I went to the market and I bought…' using noun phrases, with alliterative items in alphabetical order if you wish. Each pupil has to say the whole string, using the screwdriver to fix in the commas, then add another item and use the full stop screwdriver to fix the sentence. For example: *I went to the market and I bought an amazing apple, a bashful banana, a cheerful cat, a daring dog and some enormous eggs.*

Apply
In teaching sequences, identify opportunities where pupils could apply this learning. This could be in list poetry, for example:

In my dreams, I will find:
A crimson sunset,
A curling wave,
A silver-horned unicorn

Or instructions:

You will need:
Some white paper, six paperclips, some sticky back plastic and a toilet roll tube.

Activity 2.12: A web of words Resources: word web (p. 98)	Terminology for pupils: *noun* *adjective* *suffix*

The purpose of this activity is to:

- understand how adding suffixes to a word can change the meaning and/or the word class (e.g. *happy – happiness, climb – climber, play – playful*) and how nouns can be formed by compounding.

Teach
Show pupils the word web in the Resources section and explain how it is created by adding suffixes such as *-ness, -er, -ful, -less, -er, -est* (and revise the prefix *-un* for opposites). Start with a word that is an adjective (e.g. happy) and by adding to it, show how many other words you can create. Explain that when words have the same root like this, we can call them *word families*. Link to spelling work to reinforce where spelling has to change when the ending is added.

Look at the words created with pupils. How many are adjectives? How many are nouns? How do we know? Explain that some of them will be other words but they should just look for nouns and adjectives. Test pupil's responses by:

- trying out nouns in subject or object position (e.g. *Happiness was everywhere*)
- trying out expanding noun phrases by putting adjectives before nouns.

Practise
Provide pupils with other words for making word webs. Remind them of the different ways to add the suffixes and get them to experiment. Ask them to identify a word that they think is an adjective. Give them a noun phrase and ask them to put in their adjective. Does it work? For example: *The ________ dog; The playful dog.*

Apply
Using their word webs, ask pupils to write as many sentences as they can with the adjectives and nouns they have created, plus any other words they want. For example:
*The **climber** climbed the cliff. The **climb** was very difficult.*
*There was a **playful** monkey in the **play**.*

Activity 2.13: Word combinations Resources: chart of compound nouns (p. 98), examples of German compound nouns	Terminology for pupils: *noun* *compound*

The purpose of this activity is to:

- understand how nouns can be formed by compounding.

Teach
Explain that some nouns are formed by putting two nouns together. Give some common examples, for example *playground, whiteboard, cloakroom.* Give pupils the chart from the Resources section and model combining two different words to make a compound noun. Explain that in German, many nouns are made in this way. Use the example of the German compound noun Strassenbahnhaltestelle (streetrailwaystopplace = tram stop).

Practise
Give pupils one minute to generate a list of as many nouns as possible. They should run through their list with a partner. Then ask the pairs to create their own compound noun and a definition for what it means.

Strand 3: Adverbials

Y1	**Adverbials**	
National Curriculum content: None at Y1		Terminology for pupils: None at Y1
There are no assessment criteria at Y1, but in order to understand how to express position and time, pupils need to understand the meanings of many common prepositions, including *between*, *on top of*, *afterwards*, *across*.		
Activity 3.1: Where is...? Resources: soft toy		
The purpose of this activity is to learn how to talk about where things are. **Teach** Place a soft toy or special object somewhere in the classroom and describe to pupils where it is. For example: 'I have put Barnaby on the shelf, between the paintbrushes and the water pots.' Can they see the soft toy? What made it easy to find? Discuss the words you said that helped them. Ask them: 'Where should I put Barnaby now?' Pupils should give you exact instructions with regard to position. Start collecting a list of the prepositions for position: *on*, *under*, *over*, *in front of*, *on top of*, *etc.* Once pupils have grasped the concept of locating an object that can be seen, you can move on to hiding the object completely (e.g. *inside*, *behind*). **Practise** Pupils should play the game in pairs. They could do this in the classroom or playground, or in another area of the school where there are opportunities for varying where objects are put. **Apply** Pupils should start to use prepositions in oral and written sentences to indicate place. They do not need to know the term *preposition*.		
Activity 3.2: When did...? Resources: none needed		
The purpose of this activity is to learn how to talk about when things have happened. This can link to work on past tense verbs. **Teach** Write a few sentences describing a school visit. Make sure that you include adverbials of time in initial positions in the sentence – *On Friday*, *Next*, *In the morning*, *At ten o'clock*, *Later*, *After*, etc. Use shared reading to talk about the information at the start of the sentences. Why is it useful for readers? **Practise** Ask pupils to talk about the visit. When did particular events happen? Orally create sentences to talk about the trip using these words and phrases. **Apply** Encourage pupils to use adverbial words and phrases when creating sentences orally or in writing.		

Y2	Adverbials	
National Curriculum content: • Use of *-ly* in standard English to turn adjectives into adverbs.		Terminology for pupils: *adverb*

Pupils need to:

- understand that the suffix *-ly* makes a word that describes how or when something happens (linked to the verb) in a sentence (e.g. *quickly*, *suddenly*, *happily*)
- understand that an adverb can add detail to a sentence.

Note: Continue encouraging pupils to use adverbials of place and time, adapting the Y1 activities for different text types.

Activity 3.3: Collecting adverbs Resources: examples of sentences containing adverbs from your teaching text	Terminology for pupils: *adverb*

The purpose of this activity is to:

- understand that the suffix *-ly* makes a word that describes how or when something happens (linked to the verb) in a sentence (e.g. *quickly*, *suddenly*, *happily*).

Teach

Show pupils a list of adjectives – for example, *bad*, *bold*, *foolish*, *kind*, *poor*, *rude*, *safe*, *silent*. Put some of these into sentences on the board. Discuss what these words do: describe a noun (*The* ***bold*** *knight fought the dragon*).

Show pupils that if we add the suffix *-ly* to these words, they can be used in a different way. They no longer make sense in the adjective position, but they can go in a different position in the sentence. For example, *The* ***boldly*** *knight fought the dragon* does not make sense, but we can say *The knight fought the dragon* ***boldly***. Discuss with pupils whether this word still describes the knight and explain the difference: these words describe the verb/action, rather than the noun. These are called *adverbs* and they occupy a separate slot in the sentence.

Find examples of adverbs in the text you are using, or books pupils are reading, and start an adverb collection.

Note: Pupils will also need to understand that some single-word adverbs do not end in *-ly*. For example, we cannot add *-ly* to good to make an adverb and *good* itself is not an adverb, so we can't say *He did it good*. We have to use *well* in this instance. This links with work on Standard English. In the same way, *fast* is an alternative to *quickly*, *rapidly* and *speedily*.

Practise

In pairs, pupils should look at some sentences containing adverbs. Between them, they should talk about which word is the adverb and explain what it is doing. What verb is it describing?

Apply

Pupils should choose some sentences from the narrative they are writing and add adverbs to provide their reader with information on *how* the action was happening.

Activity 3.4: Adjectives to adverbs Resources: examples of adverbs ending in *-fully* (pages 99–100)	Terminology for pupils: *adverb*

The purpose of this activity is to:

- understand that the suffix *-ly* makes a word that describes how or when something happens (linked to the verb) in a sentence (e.g. *quickly*, *suddenly*, *happily*).

Teach
Recap how nouns are transformed into adjectives with the suffix *-ful*. Then remind pupils how an adjective is changed into an adverb by adding the suffix *-ly*. Look at an adjective that ends in *-ful* (e.g. *careful*, *hopeful*). Demonstrate that when we want to transform these words into adverbs, we simply add *-ly* – nothing changes in the adjective. Make sure pupils understand that this means a double *l* pattern in these adverbs.

Practise
Provide pupils with examples of adverbs ending *-fully* from the grid in the Resources section. They should work in pairs to identify the boundary between the adjective and the adverb. They should then talk about the meanings of these words and share with the class.

Apply
Encourage pupils to use this type of adverb correctly in their writing.

Activity 3.5: Transform! Resources: *A Dog's Day* PDF	Terminology for pupils: *adverb*

The purpose of this activity is to:

- understand that the suffix *-ly* makes a word that describes how or when something happens (linked to the verb) in a sentence (e.g. *quickly*, *suddenly*, *happily*)
- understand that when adjectives end in *y*, we need to change the *y* to an *i* before adding *-ly* to make an adverb.

Teach
Recap how an adjective can be changed into an adverb by adding the suffix *-ly*. Look at the examples of *happily* and *hungrily* in *A Dog's Day*. What has happened here? See if pupils can problem-solve and explain. Go through the process of changing *y* to *i* before adding *-ly*. Ask pupils to think of as many adjectives as possible ending in *y* (e.g. *happy*, *angry*, *lazy*, *merry*, *shaky*, *speedy*). Provide examples if they struggle.

Practise
Give pupils cards with a mixture of adjectives on them, some ending in *y*. Ask pupils to sort them into two piles – those that end in *y* and those that don't – and then change them all into adverbs.

Apply
Re-read a section of narrative that they have been writing. Are there any sentences where they could add adverbs to improve the information for their reader? They should now be able to transform any adjective to an adverb.

Activity 3.6: Physical sentences Resources: saw from *Sentence Toolkit*, A4 cards with clause elements on them, cards from the diagnostics set (pages 122–130)	Terminology for pupils: *adverb*

The purpose of this activity is to:

- understand that an adverb can add detail to a sentence. (Adverbs can be moved to different positions in a sentence to vary writing and create effects for the reader.)

Teach
Introduce the saw from the *Sentence Toolkit* as the tool we use for adverbs. Explain that this is because we can separate (cut) a sentence into different parts and the adverbs can then be moved around. Use the idea of different slots from Activity 1c.3, where different cards contain different clause elements: subject, verb, object and adverbial. Have some A4 cards (which can be colour coded) written out containing a sentence which fits with your teaching sequence content. For example: *Bravely Ben opened the mysterious door.*

Model that this sentence has been 'cut up' with the saw and we can now experiment to see if we can put the adverb in different places. Each card should be held by a pupil and the class can investigate where the adverb can be put. Discuss sense with them and the differences that movement makes.

Practise
In pairs or threes, use cards from the diagnostic set to experiment with creating sentences and moving the adverb to different positions. Discuss the different sentences created, which construction they prefer and why.

Apply
Look at some sentences they have written recently where they have used an adverb. Could they move the adverb to a different position in the sentence? Do they think this would be a better sentence?

Activity 3.7: How do you do? Resources: character (subject) cards and verb cards from the set supplied for the Diagnostic activity (pages 122–124), lists of adverbs collected from previous activities	Terminology for pupils: *adverb*

The purpose of this activity is to:

- understand that an adverb can add detail to a sentence.

Teach
Choose a character card and verb card. Put these in the correct position on the board and write a sentence using them, adding an object if necessary. For example: *The little girl chased the big dog*. Ask pupils, *How might she be doing that? Can you describe how that action might be happening?* Pupils may provide examples such as *quickly*, *playfully*, *angrily*.

Use the adverbs collected from previous activities to decide with pupils whether a different adverb would be better in this sentence. Ask them questions such as:

- What is the difference between that adverb and this one?
- Which is the strongest?
- Which provides the best effect?

Practise
In pairs, pupils should select a character card and a verb card (or they could choose their own character and verb). They should use these to create a sentence and then add an adverb to describe how the character is doing the action. They should keep suggesting ideas until they come up with the most effective/original adverb, which they should then record.

Apply
Pupils should use the class collection to consider the best adverbs to use in their sentences. Their comments during guided work should reflect this 'crafting' element of writing.

Activity 3.8: Try it out! Resources: chart of pre-modifying adverbs (p. 101)	Terminology for pupils: *adverb*

The purpose of this activity is to:

- understand that an adverb can add detail to a sentence. (Introduce the use of adverbs to intensify the meaning of the adjective, e.g. *very*, *extremely*, or reduce the effect, e.g. *fairly*, *quite*. The key question word used will be *how*, since these types of adverbs usually describe how much or how often.)

Teach
Choose a sentence that includes an adjective in the noun phrase – for example *A loud noise came from the classroom*. Explain that we can use an *-ly* adverb to say how loud the noise was: *really*, *extremely*. This is also a good opportunity to introduce the idea that not all single-word adverbs end in *-ly* – we could use *very*.

Then take a sentence that includes an adjective in the complement position – for example: *It was a big surprise*. Extend previous learning to adding an adverb in this type of construction: *It was a really big surprise*. Start a collection of adverbs that can be used this way – use the chart of pre-modifying adverbs in the Resources section for ideas.

Practise
Give pupils a sentence on card to work on in pairs (this could be an example from the text you are using). For example: *The nasty witch turned the prince into a frog*. Ask pupils to try out some of the adverbs they have collected and see if they can be put between *The and nasty*. They should discuss whether they make sense and which ones they think are the best.

This activity can also use the SVC structures – for example: *The prince was angry*.

Apply
Ask pupils to look at the writing in their most recent unit of work. Have they used any of these adverbs? Challenge them to add an adverb into one sentence.

Pupils should start to experiment with these adverbs in their writing where appropriate.

Activity 3.9: Advise and instruct Resources: *Super Cool Chemical Reaction Activities* PDF	Terminology for pupils: *adverb*

The purpose of this activity is to:

- understand that an adverb can add detail to a sentence. (Adverbs can help a reader by giving advice in instructions and providing sequencing.)

Teach
Show pupils pages 14–15 of *Super Cool Chemical Reaction Activities*, which contain instructions for the 'Egg-cellent Eggsperiment'. Highlight the words *Gently* and *Carefully*. What are these words doing in the text? Explain that it is helpful to give readers advice when we are writing instructions. We are the expert telling them **how** to do or make something. Adverbs can help with this.

Look at some other adverbs: *firstly*, *secondly*, *next*, *finally*. Where could these be added? Unpick how these adverbs help to give a sequence or order to the instructions.

Practise
Pupils should look at pages 12–13, at the 'Mini Magic Fire Extinguisher' experiment. There is one adverb (*slowly*). Challenge pupils to add some other adverbs to give advice and help order the instructions.

Apply
Pupils should use adverbs when writing their own instructions.

Activity 3.10: Adverb assessment (1) Resources: none needed	Terminology for pupils: *adverb*

The purpose of this activity is to assess pupils' understanding of adverbs.

Write the following question on the board:

Poppy held the baby rabbit gently in her arms.

Ask them what type of word is underlined. Is it:

A an adjective
B an adverb
C a noun
D a verb?

When they have written their answers, they should share and discuss their choice.

Activity 3.11: Adverb assessment (2) Resources: cards supplied for the Diagnostic activity	Terminology for pupils: *adverb*

The purpose of this activity is to assess pupils' understanding of adverbs.

Use the diagnostic assessment activity with groups of children or the whole class (see pages 117–121) and focus on the use of adverbials in a sentence. Build simple sentences using the colour-coded cards. Can pupils:

- suggest adverbs
- change adverbs
- swap adverbs around
- discuss what adverbs do in a sentence?

Strand 4: Verbs

Y1	**Verbs**
National Curriculum content: • **Suffixes** that can be added to **verbs** where no change is needed in the spelling of root words (e.g. *helping*, *helped*, *helper*). • How the **prefix** *un-* changes the meaning of **verbs** and adjectives (negation, for example *unkind*, or undoing: *untie the boat*).	Terminology for pupils: None at Y1

Pupils need to:

- understand that a sentence contains information about someone or something that 'does', 'is' or 'has' something
- begin to understand the concept of present and past tense, and use this understanding orally
- spell the suffixes *-ing* and *-ed*.

Pupils will need to have covered lessons 1.1 to 1.5 of the sentence strand prior to these sessions.

Activity: 4.1 Sort it!
Resources: hammer from the *Sentence Toolkit*, example sentences (p. 102)

The purpose of this activity is to:

- understand that a sentence contains information about someone or something that 'does', 'is' or 'has' something.

Teach
Use a range of sentences from Set 1 in the Resources section, or from texts you are using in the classroom. Read them out and ask pupils to 'hammer' when they hear the *doing*, *having* or *being* word. Write the sentences on the board and draw around the hammer words to highlight them. Discuss whether these words are about someone *doing* something, *being* something (e.g. *happy*, *sad*, *excited*) or having something (e.g. *a cold*, *a ball*, *a book*). Sort them into a chart that has *Doing*, *Being* and *Having* as headings.

Practise
In the hall or outside, set up three areas: one for *doing*, one for *being* and one for *having*. Read out a sentence to the class and ask them to 'hammer' the verb and then run to the area for *doing*, *being* or *having*. Try this with several sentences.

Back in the classroom, give pupils the sentences in Set 2 and, in pairs, they should sort them into verb types. As a class, discuss how the sentences have been sorted. Create a chart for the wall and start to collect verbs for each category.

Apply
Pupils should choose sentences from books they are reading, write them out and place them on the wall chart.

Activity 4.2: Verb bingo Resources: wall chart created in Activity 4.1, bingo cards (p. 103)	

The purpose of this activity is to:

- understand that a sentence contains information about someone or something that 'does', 'is' or 'has' something.

Teach

Look back at the wall chart created during and after the last session. What do pupils notice about the verbs in each category? Identify that in the *being* section the verbs are all *is*, *was*, *were*, *are*, *am* and that in the *having* section they are all *had*, *has*, *have*.

Practise and apply

Give each pupil a bingo card from the Resources section, containing *being*, *having*, *doing*. Read out a range of sentences from the wall chart, the cards used in Activity 4.1 and pupils' books. When you have read them out, place them on the board. Pupils should mark off on their bingo cards when sentences of particular types are read out. Once a pupil shouts 'Bingo!', go through the sentences with the class to check that they are right.

Activity 4.3: Past and present Resources: *Playing with Friends* PDF or other texts that show the past and present tenses clearly, hammer from the *Sentence Toolkit*	

The purpose of this activity is to:

- begin to understand the concept of present and past tense, and use this understanding orally
- spell the suffixes *-ing* and *-ed*.

This session would link well to a history topic that the pupils are studying.

Teach

Read the book to the class and discuss what is important about playing with friends for them, to ensure they have engaged with the meaning of the text. Re-read the sentences and 'hammer' the verbs. Record the verbs on the board under the headings 'past' and 'present'. What do pupils notice about the verbs? Discuss the endings of the words. Stick to regular verbs wherever possible.

Practise

Bring a range of objects into the classroom from the past and the present – for example, a satchel, a slate, a rucksack, an iPad, or use images from another book in the *Comparing Past and Present* series. Discuss the old items and use the sentence pattern *In the past… and today…* . In pairs, pupils should create the past and present sentences orally. Practise saying them with actions for the capital letter and punctuation and then share with the whole class. The class should 'hammer' when they hear the verb (*doing*, *being* or *having*). Record the verbs on the board and discuss the endings for the past and present.

Apply

Pupils should write their own sentences for a pair of objects.

Activity 4.4: Adding *-ed* Resources: verb matrix (p. 104)	

The purpose of this activity is to:

- spell the suffixes *-ing* and *-ed*.

Teach
Look at the verbs collected for the past and present. What do pupils notice about the verbs used in the past (work with regular verbs only at this point). Handwrite *-ed* several times with the correct joins.

Choose a verb from the matrix in the Resources section, change it into the past tense, then write it down. Explain to pupils that if the verb has a short vowel when you add *-ed*, then the final consonant is doubled (*shopped*, *stopped*, *rubbed*, *knitted*).

Practise
In pairs, pupils should choose verbs from the matrix, convert them into the past tense and then write them. Check spellings as a whole class. Revise doubling the consonant where there is a short vowel.

Apply
Pupils can look back at the sentences they wrote in the previous activity and check whether they spelt them correctly, particularly the *-ed* part.

In pairs, they should take it in turns to choose a verb and create a sentence. They should then both write the sentence and check each other's work to see if they have spelt the verb correctly.

Each time you share a book with pupils, pick out a few sentences to explore whether it is written in the past or present tense.

Activity 4.5: Assessment: silly sentences Resources: image from a recent text	

The purpose of this activity is to assess pupils' understanding of verbs in the past and present tense.

In pairs, pupils orally create a series of sentences based around an image. These sentences should include the actions for capital letters and full stops. Each pair should read their sentences to the rest of the class, who identify the verbs by 'hammering', then decide whether the sentence is in the past or present.

Y2	**Verbs**
National Curriculum content: • Correct choice and consistent use of **present tense** and **past tense** throughout writing. • Use of the **progressive** form of **verbs** in the **present** and **past tense** to mark actions in progress (for example, *she is drumming, he was shouting*).	Terminology for pupils: *verb* *tense (present, past)* *present progressive* *past progressive* *apostrophe*

Pupils need to:

- understand that any verb can be written in a different tense
- be able to identify if a verb is written in the past or present tense
- understand that the verb in a sentence is frequently more than one word (a verb phrase)
- understand that there are different ways of expressing the past and present tenses (e.g. past simple and past progressive: *he ran, he was running*; present simple and present progressive: *he runs, he is running*)
- know how to use the verb *to be* to create progressive forms
- maintain choice of tense throughout writing for cohesion.

Activity 4.6: Hammer those verbs! Resources: sentence cards (p. 104), verb and tense spotter text (p. 105)	Terminology for pupils: *verb* *tense (past and present)*

The purpose of this activity is to:

- understand that any verb can be written in a different tense
- be able to identify if a verb is written in the past or present tense.

Teach
Choose sentences from a range of texts in the past and present simple form. Review finding the verb by 'hammering' when you hear the *doing/being/having* word. Encourage pupils to use the term *verb* when they hammer. For pupils who can find verbs in sentences, challenge them by giving sentences of more than one clause and asking them to identify all the verbs. How do we know if a verb is in the past or present tense? Take ideas and record them on the board. Model exploring sentences and categorise them into past and present tense.

Practise
Give pupils copies of the sentence cards from the Resources section. In pairs, pupils should take it in turns to read a sentence to their partner. Their partner 'hammers' out the verb and then underlines it in the sentence. They should say whether it is in the past or present tense and how they know. Review what pupils have done.

Apply
Provide pupils with a short piece of text. Ask them to circle all the verbs and then say whether the text is in the past or present and why. An example from *Sabretooth Cats* is provided in the Resources section but you will need to use other texts to match pupils' reading attainment.

Activity 4.7: What are you doing? Resources: photos of the class doing activities in the playground, dining room or assembly hall	Terminology for pupils: *verb* *tense (past and present)*

The purpose of this activity is to:

- understand that the verb in a sentence is frequently more than one word (a verb phrase)
- understand that there are different ways of expressing the past and present tenses (e.g. past simple and past progressive: *he ran, he was running*; present simple and present progressive: *he runs, he is running*)
- know how to use the verb *to be* to create progressive forms.

Teach

Take photos of the class in the playground at playtime and lunchtime for use in this lesson. Ask questions such as *What is Ben doing?* Record the answers that pupils give. Because pupils are looking at pictures of something that happened before, some may give the answers in the simple form (*he ran*) and some in the progressive form (*he was running*).

Choose one of the past progressive sentences and convert it to the past simple. Ask pupils why they did not answer in this tense. You are looking for responses about the on-going nature of the event.

Practise

Use another few pictures of the pupils in different circumstances, such as in the assembly or dining hall. In pairs, ask pupils to label the images with sentences that describe what is going on in the picture. They can be in the simple or progressive form.

Apply

Get pairs to swap sentences and underline the verbs in the other pair's sentences. Use this as an assessment activity for the next session.

Activity 4.8: All in agreement Resources: conjugation table and cards with *am/is/are/was/were*, cloze paragraph (pages 105–106)	Terminology for pupils: *verb* *tense (past and present)* *present progressive*

The purpose of this activity is to:

- understand that the verb in a sentence is frequently more than one word (a verb phrase)
- understand that there are different ways of expressing the past and present tenses (e.g. past simple and past progressive: *he ran, he was running*; present simple and present progressive: *he runs, he is running*)
- know how to use the verb *to be* to create progressive forms.

Teach

Using the past progressive sentences that pupils created in Activity 4.7, write the verbs on the board so that pupils can see how they are constructed. Draw attention to the two words that make up the verb form. Pupils will notice that the auxiliary verb is in the past tense (*was, were*) and the main verb has *-ing* on the end in all cases.

Model creating the auxiliary verb by conjugating the verb *to be* with the pupils, using the table in the Resources section. You may want to link to apostrophes for contraction here for *it's* and *they're*.

Practise

Give pairs of pupils cards with *am, is, are, were* on them. Call out a pronoun and ask pupils to hold up the card with the correct verb to make the subject and verb agree.

Apply

Give pupils a copy of the cloze paragraph from the Resources section. Ask them to write in the correct form of *to be* in the past tense in the gaps. Ask whether it is possible to complete this in the present tense and why.

Activity 4.9: Simple to progressive Resources: example sentence in the past simple and progressive forms	Terminology for pupils: *verb* *tense (past and present)* *present progressive*

The purpose of this activity is to:

- understand that the verb in a sentence is frequently more than one word (a verb phrase)
- understand that there are different ways of expressing the past and present tenses (e.g. past simple and past progressive: *he ran, he was running*; present simple and present progressive: *he runs, he is running*)
- know how to use the verb *to be* to create progressive forms.

Teach

Read out the sentences that pupils created in previous sessions and 'hammer' when they hear the verbs. Write the sentences on the board and underline the verbs. Discuss the simple and progressive forms and point out that some have only one word (*ran*) and in others the verb consists of two words (*was running*). Convert a sentence in the past simple into the past progressive. Where are the verbs? What difference does it make? When might you use each form?

Practise

Give pupils a range of sentences in the past simple and ask them to convert them into the progressive form. Discuss the effect that this has.

Activity 4.10: Tense sorting Resources: example sentences in the past and present progressive forms (p. 107)	Terminology for pupils: *verb* *tense (past and present)* *present progressive*

The purpose of this activity is to:

- understand that the verb in a sentence is frequently more than one word (a verb phrase)
- know how to use the verb *to be* to create progressive forms.

Teach

Use a sentence in the progressive form – for example, *Katie was reading about cowgirls*. Underline the verb and ask the pupils to show you which part of the verb gives you the tense and which gives you the meaning of what happened. The *was* gives you the tense (past) and the *reading* is what Katie was doing. Look at other sentences in the progressive form and decide which tense they are.

Practise

Give pairs of pupils a series of sentences in the progressive form from the Resources section. Ask them to underline the verb and then work out which tense the verb is in. They should then join up with another pair and see if they have the same answers.

Activity 4.11: Tense choices Resources: example texts with inconsistent tenses (p. 108)	Terminology for pupils: *verb* *tense (past and present)*

The purpose of this activity is to:

- maintain choice of tense throughout writing for cohesion.

Teach

Use a short text which has inconsistent tense choices, either from the Resources section or from pupils' own writing. Model reading through and identifying the verbs and the tense they are in. Explain that stories are usually written in the past tense and therefore *all* the verbs need to be in the past. Go through and make changes as necessary.

Practise

Pupils should work in pairs on another small piece of text that is not a narrative. An example is given in the Resources section. Identify the verbs and then check the tenses. Ensure that they are all the same tense. Share the changes made as a class.

Apply

Identify a short section in pupils' books when you mark them for pairs to go back through and check the consistency of tense. You will need to do this many times throughout the year on writing from both English and across the curriculum.

Activity 4.12: Verb assessment Resources: none needed	Terminology for pupils: *verb* *tense (past and present)*

The purpose of this activity is to assess pupils' understanding of verbs in the past and present tense.

Ask pupils to complete the following questions.

1 Write one word on the line below to complete the sentence in the **past tense**.

I ____________ to Scotland during the school holidays.

2 Circle the **verbs** in the sentence below.

Yesterday was the school sports day and Jo wore her new running shoes.

3 Write down whether each sentence is in the **past tense** or the **present tense**.

Becky was thinking.
I am reading my book.
Jo is going for a walk.

Share answers and discuss which are right and why.

Teaching resources

Strand 1a: Simple sentences

Activity 1a.2 Hammer those verbs!

Activity 1a.4 Silly sentences

the elephant	a large cake	dogs
my mum	my trousers	people
the girl	custard	sausages
the door	Queen Elizabeth	

is sitting	is	eat (s)
played	were	dropped
is chasing	tricked	was
like (s)	opened	tickled
lost	hungry	happy
lonely	excited	angry

Activity 1a.5 Sort it!

the boy is happy	is angry
my mum	red balloon
Mandy painted the door	is watching
Ben was happy	the dog sat
Rosie ran downstairs	the little brown dog

Strand 1b: Co-ordination and subordination

Activity 1b.1 Likes/dislikes

eating chocolate	worms for tea	playing football
playing in the park	washing up	tidying the bedroom
tests	fish fingers	cats
dogs	horses	holidays
walking in the rain	colouring	bedtime

Activity 1b.2: Physical sentences

and
and
and

Some plants have one flower.
Some plants have lots of flowers.
Some flowers look like a ball.
Some flowers look like a heart.
Some flowers look like a star.
Some flowers look like a bell.
Plants are living things.
Plants have many parts.
Plants need water to grow.
Plants need sunlight and air to grow.
Many plants grow flowers.

Some plants have lots of flowers.
Flowers make seeds.
New plants grow from seeds.
A petal is one part of a flower.
Some flowers have red petals.
Some flowers have purple petals.
Some flowers have patterns on their petals.
Hummingbirds and butterflies get food from flowers.
Bees get food from flowers.
Flowers make seeds.
Seeds grow and become new plants.

Activity 1b.4: Physical sentences

The boy skated down the hill.
The boy couldn't stop.
The boy looked worried.
The boy held out his hands.

Red Riding Hood sentences:

She had raven-black hair.
She had bright blue eyes.
She didn't like the forest.
She didn't like the dark.
She really enjoyed visiting Granny.
She was a bit naughty.
She was very clever.

and
but
or

Activity 1b.5: Subordinating with physical sentences

Summer days can reach 40 degrees Celsius.
It is hard to keep cool in Africa.

Above ground, meerkats stay near their holes.
They dive in when danger is near.

Meerkats dig burrows with their long, sharp claws.
They fold their ears back so sand cannot get in.

They get wet and cold.
Pups can die.

because
if
when

Subordinate clauses:
If a kestrel sees an animal to eat…
If he took one more step…
When winter comes…
When I feel afraid…
Because moles live underground…
Because of your kindness…

Activity 1b.6: Using *that*

A salamander's legs are so short.
Its belly drags on the ground.
that

Sentences joined with:	
and, but, or	*because, when, if, that*

Activity 1c.3: Fill in the slots

Who is doing/ being/having	**What happens**	**To whom or what**
Subject	***Verb***	***Object/complement***
I	like	chocolate ice cream
meerkats	dig	burrows
Rosie	noticed	some wet paw prints
lazy sloths	are	nocturnal
giraffes	eat	leaves

Activity 1c.4: Question it

what	**when**	**where**
why	**who**	**how**

can	**will**	**may**
do	**are**	

?	**?**	**?**

Activity 1c.6: How tricky this is!

How strange!	**What a lovely girl!**
How horrid!	**What magical horns!**
How difficult!	**What an unusual hat!**

Activity 1c.7: More exclamations

How +	Adjective	(+ verb)	What+	a/an+	adjective	(+ verb)

It is a perfect day.
The shoe shop was a mess.
I can smell lots of good things.
The fountain looked perfect.
I'm hungry.

Strand 2: Nouns and noun phrases

Activity 2.1: All in a name

pencils	books	door
tray	whiteboard	window
Mr	Mrs/Miss	table
toys	globe	coats
carpet	chair	sink
pens		

hospital	bag	book
London	America	houses
coat	England	eggs
China	table	apples
car	lions	Bob
foxes	Prince William	mouse
Lucy	ball	

Activity 2.2: Grammar goggles

The lion chased the mouse.
Princess Emerald gobbled up the cakes.
The dog barked.
Ben tickled the kitten.
The kitten scratched Ben.
The girls put on their coats.
Elephants eat doughnuts.

the boys	cooked
gorillas	is/are crawling
the pancakes	gobbled
Billy Baggs	is/are hiding
the tiny hamster	hug (s)
the teacher	was/were bouncing on
my cat	like (s)
giants	wobble (s)

Activity 2.4: Understanding opposites

happy	unhappy	kind
helpful	unhelpful	lucky
easy	hard	noisy
strong	weak	hot
tiny	enormous	tasty
unkind	unlucky	quiet
cold	disgusting	

Opposite sentences:

Once there was a tiny mouse which lived with a beautiful princess.

The princess was very happy as the mouse was kind and helpful.

One hot day the mouse went fishing and caught a tasty fish.

The unlucky fish begged the clever mouse to let him go.

Activity 2.5: Revise nouns

Fruit and vegetables	Toys	Girls' names	Boys' names	Animals	Countries

Activity 2.6: Expanding nouns

Their strong bodies had big muscles and short tails.
The cat's two long teeth were called canines.
These sharp, 18-centimetre teeth could cut through tough skin.

Pre-modification chart:

Determiner	Adjective	Noun
a, an, the, this, that, these, those, some, any my, our, your his, her, their, several, few, next, first, six, twelve	enormous spiky furry stripy deadly dangerous extraordinary fierce sharp scaly	dinosaur dragon tiger tail paws horns

Activity 2.7: Playing with pronouns

The huge, hairy monster ate six scrumptious goblins.
(He/She ate them.)
These fierce big cats liked chasing slow, lumbering mammoths.
My big sister gave the game to her best friend.
Your greedy dad took the last iced cake.
My cousin and I watched our dads play a really exciting football match.
Katie told Ben about the amazing, old castle.
The little old man put on a bright yellow pair of wellies.

Cloze paragraph:

____________________ eat for up to 19 hours a day! ____________________ munch mostly on ____________________. ____________________ also eat bark, leaves and roots. A zebra's ____________________ does not contain many nutrients. ____________________ has to eat a lot to get the energy ____________________ needs.

it	they	food	grass	they	it	zebras

Activity 2.9: All about apostrophes

Zebras eat for up to 19 hours a day! They munch mostly on grass. They also eat bark, leaves and roots. A zebras food does not contain many nutrients. It has to eat a lot to get the energy it needs. A zebras teeth never stop growing. Luckily all that grazing wears down their teeth. Teeth also come in handy for scratching and biting. A pair of zebras will clean each others coats by nibbling them! They also swish away flies with a flick of their tails.

Activity 2.10: Adjective overload?

Determiner	**Adjective**	**Noun**

Activity 2.11: I went to the market

My true love gave to me six swans a-swimming five gold rings four calling birds three French hens two turtle doves and a partridge in a pear tree.

Activity 2.12: A web of words

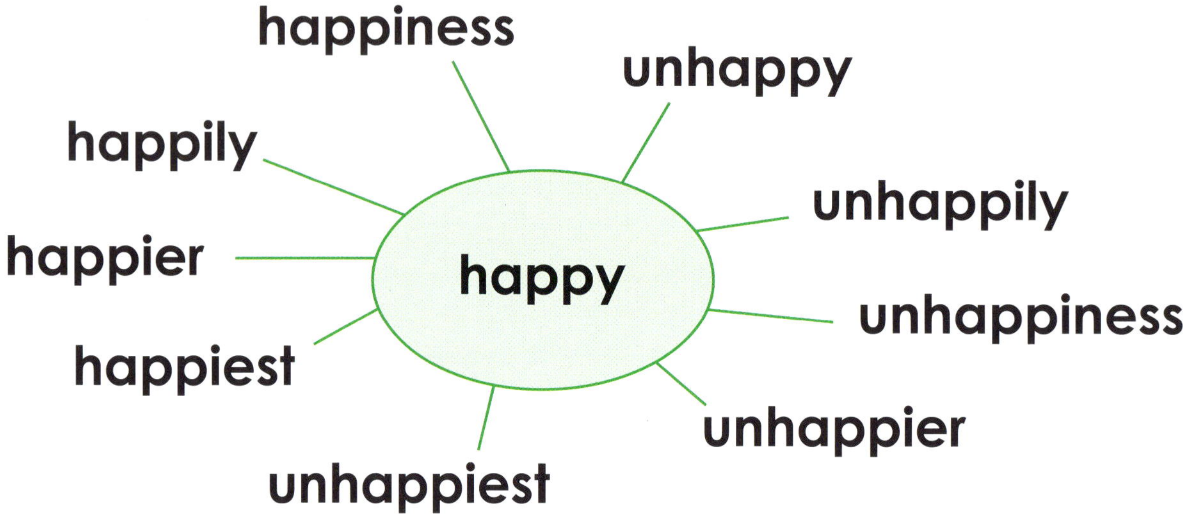

Activity 2.13: Word combinations

black	skate
life	super
moon	back
tooth	sun
butter	eye
ball	bone
paste	boat
man	light
bird	fly
flower	board

Strand 3: Adverbials

Activity 3.4: Adjectives to adverbs

awfully	bashfully	beautifully
boastfully	carefully	cheerfully
colourfully	deceitfully	delightfully
disgracefully	doubtfully	dreadfully
faithfully	fearfully	forcefully
forgetfully	frightfully	gleefully
gracefully	gratefully	harmfully
helpfully	hopefully	joyfully
meaningfully	mistrustfully	mournfully

neglectfully	painfully	peacefully
playfully	powerfully	purposefully
regretfully	remorsefully	resentfully
respectfully	rightfully	shamefully
sinfully	sorrowfully	soulfully
spitefully	stressfully	successfully
tearfully	thankfully	thoughtfully
truthfully	tunefully	unfaithfully
unhelpfully	unsuccessfully	untruthfully
usefully	wonderfully	wrongfully

Activity 3.8: Try it out!

absolutely	awfully	badly	completely
dearly	deeply	dreadfully	enormously
especially	exceedingly	extremely	fairly
greatly	hardly	hugely	largely
massively	nearly	perfectly	poorly
powerfully	pretty	quite	rather
really	remarkably	simply	slightly
strongly	surprisingly	terribly	totally
tremendously	unbelievably	very	wonderfully

Strand 4: Verbs

Activity 4.1: Sort it!

Set 1
New plants grow from seeds.
I have fingers and toes.
Bees get food from flowers.
Spiders live in the jungle.
Toads hide under rocks.
They were busy in school.
The dog was brown and fluffy.
Rosie chased the butterfly.
He has a pet dog.

Set 2
The cat ran up the tree.
He has an Xbox.
We like the beach.
Parrots live in the jungle.
They were funny.
Pupils walk to school.
I am hungry.
The Queen lives in a palace.
She has a toy car.

Activity 4.2: Verb bingo

doing	having
being	being
having	being

doing	having
having	doing
being	being

being	doing
having	being
doing	having

Activity 4.4: Adding *-ed*

play jump hunt live shop rub stop knit	ed

Activity 4.6: Hammer those verbs!

Penguins find all their food at sea.	She peeled the sandwich off the path and flew to the top of the tree.
I sat at the table.	A boy on a scooter raced by and he jumped out of the way.
There at the door stood a long line of strange creatures.	Huge tyres turn these trucks into monsters.
All rabbits do is hop.	Henry thought for a moment.
Cats get stuck up in trees all the time.	Toads catch slugs and other small animals.

Sabretooth cats roamed North and South America 10,000 years ago. They lived in grasslands and forests. The world was cooler then. Sabretooth cats were about 1 metre tall. Their strong bodies had big muscles and short tails. Females and males were the same size.

Activity 4.8: All in agreement

	Present	**Past**
I	am	was
He/she/it	is	was
you	are	were
we	are	were
they	are	were

am	**was**
is	**were**
are	

We ______________________ running down the hill when we spotted a large elephant in the garden. It ______________________ grey and had wrinkles that showed its age. We stopped and ______________________ staring when an old lady came out of the house. She ____________________ busy with buckets and cabbages and we saw that she ______________________ going to feed the elephant. 'What ____________________ you two doing?' she shouted. 'Nothing,' we replied and carried on running.

Activity 4.10: Tense sorting

Katie was reading about cowgirls.	He is hunting for his food before night falls.
Joe was riding his bike through the mountains when he had a puncture.	We were following the bus when it stopped quickly.
The penguin is looking for fish.	I was getting hungry.
She was rushing so quickly that she knocked Ravi over.	I am not listening to my big sister ever again.
I am listening to my Mum.	

Activity 4.11: Tense choices

Once upon a time, there lives a beautiful panda called Pandarella. She lived with her stepmother and two stepsisters. They are very unkind and made her do all the work in the house. One day, a messenger bring an invitation from the royal palace. The prince had invited them all to the ball. But the stepsisters tell Pandarella she cannot go.

Ladybird

The work animals do naturally often helps humans. Ladybirds can eaten up to 50 aphids in a single day. Ladybirds is small insects that destroyed crops. By eating aphids, ladybirds helped farmers to keep their crops healthy. A ladybird eaten more than 5,000 aphids during its lifetime.

Example teaching sequence

Writerly knowledge chart: *A Dog's Day* by Rebecca Rissman

How do I feel about the text?	How did the author do that?	Examples
A funny story told from two points of view. Dog having fun. Girl a bit worried.	• Flip the book over to see the second story. • Tell the same events but with characters feeling slightly different about it. • Dog causes mischief in the places he goes to. • Girl asks questions to find the dog. • Some expanded noun phrases.	*Big, muddy flower bed, some wet paw prints on the ground*

Key learning outcome:
write a story with two points of view

Elicitation task
Use an image of Little Red Riding Hood and the wolf. Ask pupils to generate ideas about what the wolf might think and say, and then what Little Red Riding Hood might say. Pupils could take on roles in pairs to help with this, then they could write down their thoughts if you wish.
Use the outcomes from this to adapt the medium-term plan and the national standards outcomes below.

Medium-term plan

Reading	Writing (Y2)	Grammar
Develop pleasure in reading, motivation to read, vocabulary understanding by: • recognising and joining in with predictable phrases • discussing the sequence of events in books and how items of information are related (Y2) • discovering non-fiction/ fiction books that are structured in different ways (Y2) • linking what they read or hear to their own experiences.	Consider what to write before starting by: • saying out loud what they are going to write about • composing a sentence orally before writing it. Develop writing by: • sequencing sentences to form short narratives • reading back what they have written to check that it makes sense • discussing what they have written with the teacher or other pupils • evaluating their writing with the teacher and other pupils.	Develop understanding of the concepts set out in Appendix 2 of the National Curriculum by: • beginning to punctuate sentences using a capital letter and a full stop or question mark • using a capital letter for names of people, places, days of the week, and the personal pronoun *I*. Develop understanding of the concepts set out in Appendix 2 by: • learning how to use both familiar and new punctuation correctly, including full stops, capital letters, question marks, commas for lists and apostrophes for the possessive (singular) (Y2).

Understand both the books they can already read accurately and fluently and those they listen to by: • checking that the text makes sense as they read and correcting inaccurate reading • drawing on what they already know or on background information and vocabulary provided by the teacher • discussing the significance of title and events • predicting what might happen on the basis of what they have read so far • answering and asking questions (Y2).	Develop a positive attitude towards and stamina for writing by: • writing narratives about personal experiences and those of others.	Understand how: • the grammatical patterns in a sentence indicate its function as a statement or question • expanded noun phrases describe and specify (e.g. *the blue butterfly*) (Y2). **Terminology** Y1: capital letter, singular, sentence, punctuation, full stop, question mark Y2: noun, noun phrase, statement, question, adjective, apostrophe

Spoken language
Pupils should be taught to use spoken language to develop understanding through speculating, hypothesising, imagining and exploring ideas.

Working at national standards	**Working at greater depth**
• Use expanded noun phrases to describe places (Y2). • Use capital letters, full stops and question marks appropriately. • Produce a story that shows a character's point of view. • Show how the character is feeling.	• Add more detail at appropriate points in the story.

Guided group writing targets

Group 1	Group 2	Group 3	Group 4	Group 5
Teaching			**Guided work linked to sequence**	**Learning: I can... I know... I understand...**
Familiarisation/immersion in text/analysis Use the imitate phase of the sequence to construct a writerly knowledge chart with pupils. **Imitate** Look at the front cover of the book (the dog's version) and discuss what might make a dog's day. Record ideas and then read the book. Model asking questions as you go through and encourage pupils to do so. Stop after each event and predict what might happen next. Stop at the point where Rusty has been in the fountain and discuss what the dog might do next. What clues are there? Talk through ideas in pairs and then pupils should write the next part of the story. Talk about who is telling the story.				

Read to the end of the dog's day and discuss the fact that the pages are upside down. Decide what to do and then compare the two front covers. What are pupils expecting? Read the text, stopping at various points, and see if the pupils can generate what happens next and link the two stories together. Learn and remember the bare bones of the text with one or two events, such as the meeting in the park. Use a story map that you have drawn and actions. Learn a bit from both stories, as Rosie's story uses questions. Pupils should retell the story in pairs, section by section, with one child telling Rosie's story and the other Rusty's story. How does Rosie feel in her story? Photocopy a picture of her and write around her the pupils' suggestions. Give pupils a photocopy of Rusty and ask them to write about he is feeling. Complete in pairs and then share as a class. Box up the text using a long piece of paper and drawing/writing the dog's story and Rosie's story to show how the two are linked (see example at the end of this chart). **Grammar** Look at the noun phrase *a big, muddy flower bed*. Ask pupils to identify the noun/s and what other information they have about it/them. Talk about the adjectives *big* and *muddy* and how they tell us more about the noun. On the board, write *a poodle* and then ask pupils to come up with some adjectives to tell us more about the poodle. Try several out and then choose the best one and label the picture. Label several more nouns on the page together. Give pairs of pupils a page from the book and ask them to create some noun phrases and label the page. Share examples and discuss which ones pupils like best. Orally create sentences that include the noun phrases. Encourage pupils to use the actions for capital letters and full stops. You may want pupils to record these sentences. Read the story again, but this time ask pupils to join in when Rosie asks a question. How will they know a question is being asked? Read it a couple of times so pupils can join in more fluently with the questions. Encourage pupils to include actions for the capital letter and question mark. Remember the capital letter for names as well.		

Pupils should think of a place that Rusty might go. Then, in the role of Rosie, they should ask the question (e.g. *Mr Magazine, have you seen Rusty go through your shop?*) Look at the title *A Dog's Day*. Identify the punctuation mark as an apostrophe and talk about why it is included. What do pupils think *Rosie's Day* might look like written down? Find objects in the classroom belonging to individual pupils and talk about, e.g. *Julia's pen*. Record each item. Model how to write a sentence that includes *Julia's pen* and then ask pupils to create a sentence based around *Joy's hat*. Have they got the correct punctuation and capital letters at the start and for the person's name? **Innovate** Draw up a list of two characters that pupils could tell two stories about, e.g. two friends, a teacher and a pupil, Little Red Riding Hood and the wolf, a parent and child. Record these on a list to display in the classroom. Choose one of the pairs to write a story about, e.g. teacher and pupil. Imagine a child sees the school door open. What mischievous things could they get up to (e.g. paint on the walls, knock over the musical instruments, take a bite out of all the fruit for break time)? Choose the two or three suggestions that pupils like best and ask them to set up the situations so that you can take photographs of them. With pupils, box up the story of what the child does. Use the photos and identify nouns in them. Generate adjectives to expand the noun phrase and label the first picture. Pupils should create their own labels for the other pictures. Adapt the story map to fit the new content. This can be done by putting sticky notes over parts that need to change, and drawing on them. **Shared writing** Model writing the text over a couple of days, to demonstrate the elements included in the writerly knowledge chart you have created with pupils. How might the teacher be feeling when they see the mess around the school? In pairs, pupils should act out what the pupil does and then think about what the teacher might do and say. Box up the new content and then retell the story.		

Shared writing Model re-reading the writing to check that it makes sense. Mark the writing and identify aspects that need further development. The aspects are detailed in the national standards section near the top of this chart.		
Capturing ideas **Invent** You will need to be flexible here with what pupils do. In Year 2, pupils should write both stories. In Year 1, they might write one of the stories, then tell the other. Pupils should choose the two characters that they want. If they are not story characters, they should place them in a situation (e.g. mother and child in the supermarket). Think of some mischievous things that one of the characters might do. Box up the new information and if needed, adapt the map. Teach the aspects identified at the end of the Innovate stage that need further development. Support pupils in writing the text, then revising and editing it to include the elements taught throughout the sequence. Pupils should move on to the second story when they are ready. Proofread the writing for spelling and punctuation. Publish a final version in a book that flips upside down. Compare and comment on the progress made from the elicitation task to the invent writing.		

Box up example (from the Imitate stage)

Rusty

Rusty woke up and went out through the front door	Found a muddy flower bed and rolled in it.	Smelt the butcher's shop. She wasn't pleased to see him.	Went to the shoe shop and chewed shoes. Owner wasn't pleased to see him.	Finds Rosie in the park.

Rosie

Noticed that the front door was open and that Rusty was gone.	Found a muddy flower bed.	Went to the butcher's shop and found paw prints. Butcher was not happy.	Went to the shoe shop and found chewed shoes.	Found Rusty in the park.

Assessment criteria and diagnostic activity

The statements in bold at the bottom of each section in the table below have been taken from the *2015–16 Interim teacher assessment frameworks at the end of Key Stage 1 and Key Stage 2*. The statements come from the writing criteria for pupils working at the expected standard.

The table includes information on where effective formative assessment information can be collected through the use of the grammar activities and diagnostic assessment tools. This information could be added to the range of other assessment information gathered in order to make an overall judgement about a pupil's standard in writing.

Strand 1: Different ways to construct sentences	
Y1	**Pupils need to:**
Constructing a simple sentence (or single-clause sentence) How **words** can combine to make **sentences** (orally and in writing). Sequencing **sentences** to form short narratives.	• Understand that we write in units of meaning called sentences. • Understand that a sentence contains information about someone or something that 'does', 'is' or 'has' something. It may include where, when or how this happens. • Understand that when we write a sentence, we start with a capital letter and end with a full stop. • Recognise a full stop. • Orally rehearse sentences. • Punctuate either orally or with an action. • Ask and answer questions about the information included. • Talk about the sentences they have written and why they are sentences. • Write a sequence of sentences in fiction and information.
Y1	**Pupils need to:**
Co-ordination and subordination Joining words and joining clauses using *and*.	• Understand that we can use *and* to add two words together in a sentence, when those two things are acting or being affected in the same way (e.g. *Jack and Jill went up the hill*. Both Jack and Jill are acting in the same way. *Fred was tired and hungry*). • Understand that we can join two sentences together using the word *and*. When this happens we only need one full stop at the end. • Understand that this word means we are adding information. • Understand that although these structures occur in a 'stream' in speech, it is important not to use too many clauses in one sentence. • Orally rehearse sentences. • Punctuate either orally or with an action.
Y2	**Pupils need to:**
Co-ordination and subordination **Subordination** (*when, if that, because*) and **co-ordination** (using *or, and, but*).	• Understand that we can join two sentences together using the words *and, or, but*. When this happens, we have constructed one sentence with two clauses (a compound sentence). • Understand the meaning of these conjunctions: *and* = addition, *but* = contrast, *or* = alternative. • Understand that when a subject is repeated, it can be replaced with a pronoun or omitted (e.g. *George loves chocolate but (he) hates ice cream*.) • Extend sentences using subordinating conjunctions such as *when, if, that, because* and be able to talk about how they affect the meaning of the sentence. • Understand that *when, if, because* (and others) can start sentences. **Use co-ordination (or/and/but) and some subordination (when/if/that/because).**

Y1	Pupils need to:
Sentences types Introduction to capital letters, full stops, question marks and exclamation marks to demarcate **sentences**. Capital letters for names and for the personal **pronoun**.	• Understand that there are different types of sentences, which have different end punctuation.
Y2	**Pupils need to:**
Sentence types How the grammatical patterns in a sentence indicate its function as a **statement**, **question**, **exclamation** or **command**. Use of capital letters, full stops, question marks and exclamation marks to demarcate **sentences**.	• Understand that there are different ways of forming a sentence – questions, statements, exclamations, commands – and be able to talk about what makes them different. • Understand that questions can be constructed in different ways. • Be able to tell the difference between questions and exclamations beginning with *what* and *how*. • Understand how different sentence types are punctuated. **Use different sentences with different forms in their writing (statements, questions, exclamations and commands).** **Demarcate most sentences with capital letters and full stops and with some use of question marks and exclamation marks.**

Strand 2: Nouns and noun phrases	
Y1	**Pupils need to:**
Regular **plural noun suffixes** *-s* or *-es* (for example, *dog, dogs; wish, wishes*), including the effects of these suffixes on the meaning of the noun. How the **prefix** *un-* changes the meaning of … **adjectives** (*negation*, for example, *unkind*).	• Understand what the nouns in sentences are and how to form the plurals (link to spelling teaching). • Understand that nouns can be people, places or things. • Understand that adjectives can be added to a noun to add more detail. • Understand that opposites can be created by adding the prefix *un-* to adjectives.
Y2	**Pupils need to:**
Formation of **nouns** using **suffixes** such as *-ness*, *-er* and by compounding (for example, *whiteboard*, *superman*). Formation of **adjectives** using **suffixes** such as *-ful*, *-less*. Use of the **suffixes** *-er*, *-est* in **adjectives**.	• Understand that a group of words can work together to fill the noun slot in a sentence and that this is called a *noun phrase*. • Understand that a noun phrases can be replaced with a pronoun. • Understand how to construct a noun phrase using determiners, adjectives and nouns (e.g. *My naughty, mean sister*). • Understand how commas are used in lists of adjectives and noun phrases. • Understand how adjectives can be used in different places in a sentence, such as before the noun (*My naughty sister*) and after the verb (*My sister is naughty*).

Expanded **noun phrases** for description and specification (for example, *the blue butterfly, plain flour, the man in the moon*). Commas to separate items in a list. Apostrophes to mark singular possession in nouns (for example, *the girl's name*). How hyphens can be used to avoid ambiguity (for example, *man eating shark* versus *man-eating shark*, or *recover* versus *re-cover*). (Although *hyphen* is terminology in Year 6, this punctuation mark will be used in word work and writing from Year 2 onwards).	• Understand how adding suffixes to a word can change the meaning and/or the word class (e.g. *happy – happiness, climb – climber, play – playful*) and how nouns can be formed by compounding. • Understand the difference between adding an s for a plural and adding an apostrophe s for singular possession. **Use some expanded noun phrases to describe and specify.**

Strand 3: Adverbials	
Y2	**Pupils need to:**
Use of *-ly* in standard English to turn adjectives into adverbs.	• Understand that the suffix *-ly* makes a word that describes how or when something happens (linked to the verb) in a sentence (e.g. *quickly, suddenly, happily*). • Understand that an adverb can add detail to a sentence.

Strand 4: Verbs	
Y1	**Pupils need to:**
Suffixes that can be added to **verbs** where no change is needed in the spelling of root words (e.g. *helping, helped, helper*). How the **prefix** *un-* changes the meaning of **verbs** (*undo, untie*). (Note: links to spelling and writing)	• Understand that a sentence contains information about someone or something that 'does', 'is' or 'has' something. • Begin to understand the concept of present and past tense. Use this understanding orally.

Y2	Pupils need to:
Correct choice and consistent use of **present tense** and **past tense** throughout writing. Use of the **progressive** form of **verbs** in the **present** and **past tense** to mark actions in progress (for example, *she is drumming, he was shouting*). **Apostrophes** to mark where letters are missing in spelling.	• Understand that any verb can be written in a different tense. • Be able to identify if a verb is written in the past or present tense. • Understand that the verb in a sentence is frequently more than one word (a verb phrase). • Understand that there are different ways of expressing the past and present tense e.g. past simple and past progressive (he ran, he was running), present simple and present progressive (*he runs, he is running*). • Know how to use the verb *to be* to create the progressive forms. **Use present and past tense mostly correctly and consistently.**

Diagnostic activity

The purpose of this activity is to gather information to help you make judgements against the assessment criteria. Carry out the basic diagnostic game below, using the cards and instructions, then look at the suggestions for how to extend the diagnostic activity to focus on key areas of learning for Years 1 and 2.

Terminology for pupils	
Year 1	letter, capital letter, word, singular, plural, sentence, punctuation, full stop, question mark, exclamation mark
Year 2	noun, noun phrase, statement, question, exclamation, command, compound, adjective, verb, suffix, adverb, tense (past, present), apostrophe, comma

Notes for teachers about the colour-coded cards

For this generic diagnostic activity, use only the cards listed below. For Year 1 pupils, you may use a limited set.

There are additional cards of different colours for the year group variations. Please refer to the additional games for each year group for instructions on how to use these extra cards.

All the Year 1/2 cards are based on the theme of the seaside, and pupils should be able to use them to make a range of fiction and non-fiction sentences.

The set of cards contains some noun cards (blue) with single words. You will need to remove these for the introduction to the basic diagnostic game.

Similarly, you may wish to remove the verb cards (pink) with the single words (*is*, *are*, *was*, *were*). This will prevent pupils forming sentences with complements (e.g. *A crab is a sea creature*).

Although only *-ly* adverbials are specified in the Year 2 National Curriculum, it is likely that pupils will naturally wish to use simple when/where adverbials in their writing. For this reason, a selection of these is included in the card examples. You can use these as you see fit.

You may need to change the colours of the cards according to what you have available. If this is necessary, please note:

- The colours should to be consistent each time pupils use them.
- The colours need to be consistent across the school.
- Where possible, determiners, adjectives and nouns/noun phrases should be similar shades (e.g. blues and purples to signify that they all form parts of the noun phrase).

Key to the coloured cards

Blue: nouns, noun phrases, subject and object pronouns, possessive pronouns
Pink: verbs
Green: adverbials
Yellow: conjunctions
White: punctuation

Introducing pupils to the cards

Ideally, pupils should work in groups of three to six, as the problem-solving and discussion within the group will provide useful information about how well pupils have grasped the concepts.

Give each child a blue, pink, green, yellow and white card. Ask them what is written/ what is the job of each coloured card. Give each child a chance to answer individually, then encourage them to work as a group and pool their cards. Prompt/question pupils, but do not give them the answer. Make notes about their understanding.

Explain the game to pupils. They will be working as a team initially, although you may split them into pairs as you progress. Stress that this is not an easy game – they are going to have to really think about it!

Basic diagnostic game: instructions

1. Put the blue, pink, white and green cards into piles. Keep the yellow cards to one side. Pick a blue card (noun phrase). Pupils read what is on the card.

2. Pupils should turn one pink (verb) card over. Does it work with the noun? (Use the term *noun* or refer to the blue card with Years 1–4; use the term *noun*, *subject* or *object* in Years 5–6). What about sense? Could they build a sentence with these two cards? If it doesn't work, give each child two pink cards from the pile and ask them to consider if they have any verbs that would work now. They should choose one.

3. What colour card do they need to pick next to make a sentence? Let them choose a card from one of the four piles. If the new word/phrase does not fit, let them turn over two more of the same colour to widen the choice.

4. Pupils can use up to six cards of the three main colours to make their sentence, using the white cards to add the punctuation. If you wish, introduce the scoring system below for pupils to collect points and allow them to add up their scores using a score card like the example given.

5. Introduce the yellow cards (conjunctions). Make sure pupils know what these are and what they do. Ask pupils to choose a yellow card, then extend their sentence using any other colour cards they want.

6 Discuss the sentences that they have made, using relevant terminology and probing understanding and misconceptions (e.g. punctuation, the difference between co-ordinating and subordinating conjunctions or main and subordinate clauses).

Note: Make sure you have blank cards in the colours that you are using so that pupils can add words and phrases if needed.

Record notes about pupils' understanding. Detail the knowledge that they demonstrate, such as terminology, and jot down notes from their discussion on anything that shows either good understanding or gaps in knowledge.

Scoring system

'Silly' sentence semantically (but grammatically correct) = 1 point per card + 1 for the sentence.
Grammatically correct sentence + makes sense in the genre = 1 point per card + 5 for the sense.
Correct punctuation: 1 point per correct card.
Terminology: bonus points at the teacher's discretion for correct terminology used in discussion of their sentences.
Impact: bonus points at the teacher's discretion for relevant explanations made about changes in meaning or the impact on the reader of using grammatical items in a particular way.

	Number of points
Points per card	
Sentence	
Sense	
Punctuation	
Terminology	
Impact	
Other bonus points	
Total	

Generic questions to ask about parts of sentences and punctuation

Use the following questions when you introduce each colour-coded set of cards and as you build sentences throughout the activity.

Parts of sentences:
What does this colour card do in the sentence?
What is it called?
(If it is a phrase) What is the most important word and why?
(If it is a phrase) What do the other words in the phrase do?
Can this card go anywhere else in the sentence and still make sense? Does the meaning of the sentence stay the same or change?

Punctuation:
What punctuation do you need?
What job is the punctuation doing?
Is there any other punctuation that could replace it?
If so, which could you choose and why?
Can you change the meaning by changing the punctuation?

Standard English

It is important to take every opportunity to secure pupils' understanding and use of Standard English throughout this activity. Where they demonstrate incorrect use of English or misconceptions, discuss and correct them. Common errors are likely to be subject/verb agreement (*we was playing in the park*), incorrect tense form (*he brung*) and incorrect pronoun use (*Becca and me went swimming*).

Years 1/2 variations to the diagnostic activity

The following activities offer some variations on the generic diagnostic game. They focus on specific aspects of the Programme of Study for Years 1 and 2. You do not need to use all the activities – choose and adapt those that are relevant to gather the information you need.

Key to the additional coloured cards (to be used alongside cards from the basic set)

Light blue: adjectives
Purple: determiners

Sentence types

Y2: How the grammatical patterns in a sentence indicate its function as a statement, question, exclamation or command

The sentences created using the cards will mainly be statements. Ensure that pupils can recognise what type of sentence they are. Explore questions, commands and exclamations by orally transforming the statements they have made. In each case, ask:

- What did you have to do to change the sentence?
- Do any cards move or disappear within the sentence?
- If so, which ones and why?
- What punctuation do you need for different sentence types?
- Where would you use a sentence like this? (put in context)

Noun phrases

Y1/2: Expanded noun phrases for description and specification; commas to separate items in a list; how hyphens can be used to avoid ambiguity

1 Use the single-word noun cards (blue), adjective cards (light blue), determiner cards (purple), verb cards (pink) and punctuation cards (white) and sort them into piles.

2 Ask pupils to choose one card from each pile to make a sentence. Then ask them to change the determiner (purple) card. How does this change the sentence? Repeat several times to explore the differences in meaning, using the determiners.

3 Introduce the adjective cards (light blue). Ask pupils to choose adjectives to add to their sentences and any punctuation that they might need. Discuss their choices and what job the adjectives do in the sentence.

Verbs

Y2: Correct choice and consistent use of present tense and past tense; use of the progressive form of the verbs in the present and past tense to mark actions in progress

Use the sentences that pupils have created to look at the impact on meaning of changing the verb tense and form. In the verb card set there are examples of verbs in the present simple, present progressive, past simple and past progressive. Explore the effect of changing the tense (present to past) and the form (changing from the simple to the progressive). You will need blank pink cards so that you or pupils can write variations of the verbs used in their original sentences.

Y2: Using verbs in sentences with complements. Although there are no specific requirements to teach this in the National Curriculum, it is important in understanding how verbs work in sentences. Refer to the Subject knowledge section for further information.

Use the verb cards (pink) with *is*, *are*, *was*, *were*, single-word noun cards (blue), determiner cards (purple) and the adjective cards (light blue). Ask pupils to build a noun phrase by choosing a single noun, determiner and adjective. Then ask them to choose one of the verb cards and ask them if they can rearrange the cards so that they make a simple sentence (e.g. *The red bucket*, *The bucket is red*.) Discuss which word the verb is and talk to pupils to check their understanding that verbs are *being*, *having* and *doing* words.

Nouns: single-word (print or copy on blue card)

net	sun	dog
boy	girl	sand
rock	fish	crab
bucket	spade	rock pools
Jack	Molly	kite
bucket	spade	rock pools
wind	deckchair	shell
seaweed	beach	water
boats	beach-hut	waves
sea	sandcastle	ball
cave	pebbles	ice-creams

Noun phrases (print or copy on blue card)

the boy	the blue sea	a little girl
Dad	a plastic spade	the family
white waves	a big sandcastle	the picnic
lots of pretty shells	a yellow starfish	tiny, shiny fish
dark green seaweed	her sun hat	speed boats
the rock pool	the tired donkey	the shark
a fishing boat	an ice-cream with a flake	two dolphins
surfers	Mum's beach towel	a greedy seagull
the big dog	a green beach ball	the life guard
happy children	the fishing net	crabs with sharp claws

Verbs: simple present/simple past (print or copy on pink card)

have	hides	hide
lives	live	find
finds	see	sees
run	runs	float
floats	swim	swims
set off	floated	flew
rode	swam	crept
peered	chased	disappeared
searched (for)	opened	dipped
is	are	has
was	were	had

Verbs: present progressive/past progressive (print or copy on pink card)

is fishing	is standing	is running
is chasing	is escaping	is floating
is watching	is eating	is sitting
are playing	are rescuing	are sitting
are catching	are scurrying	are hiding
are building	are swimming	are racing
was riding	was digging	was splashing
was crashing	was bobbing	was searching (for)
was carrying	was plodding	was snatching
were eating	were splashing	were dipping
were collecting	were shouting	were building
were playing	were sheltering	were throwing

Adverbials (print or copy on green card)

quickly	quietly	slowly
happily	sadly	carefully
gently	angrily	curiously
loudly	playfully	suddenly
silently	secretly	greedily
beautifully	magically	lazily

home	off	away
well	now	soon
today	yesterday	

Adverbial phrases (print or copy on green card)

along the beach	into the waves
on the sand	in the cold sea water
under the deckchair	in the rock pools
in the breeze	on the sandcastle
with his net	at the beach
next to the ice-cream hut	behind the rocks
under the bucket	in the sunshine
that afternoon	this morning
on Saturday	at sunset
very fast	with a swoop

Conjunctions (print or copy on yellow card)

and	and	and
but	but	but
because	if	as soon as
after	before	until
as	when	

Punctuation (print or copy on white card)

.	.	.
.	CL (capital letter)	CL (capital letter)
CL (capital letter)	CL (capital letter)	,
,	,	?
?	!	!

Adjectives (print or copy on light blue card)

deep	happy	dark
big	sunny	hot
lucky	blue	golden
soft	unhappy	cold
shiny	old	long
enchanted	clear	beautiful
deepest	brave	strange
great	kind	tiny
freezing	huge	terrified
fierce	young	amazed
darkest	highest	special

Determiners (print or copy on purple card)

a	an	the
a	an	the
a	an	the
a	an	the
that	this	my
his	her	all
one	your	their
many	two	three

Appendix

Additional subject knowledge (alphabetically arranged)

Adjectival phrases

We are familiar with using adjectives or strings of adjectives in front of a noun to create a noun phrase. In this type of phrase, the noun is the head word. For example, *the lazy, luminous, long-tailed lizard* contains the adjectives *lazy, luminous* and *long-tailed*, and these are pre-modifying the head word in the phrase which is the noun 'lizard'.

Adjectival phrases are phrases in which the adjective is the head of the phrase, as in the following examples:

- *The princess was **very beautiful**.*
- *The policeman's hunch proved **entirely correct**.*
- *The strong wind made the pupils **quite crazy**.*

Complements

Complements are one of the five clause elements and are probably the least familiar to primary teachers. The words in the complement positions provide information about the subject or object in the sentence, and can be an adjective/adjective phrase, noun/noun phrase, or a clause with a nominal function.

- Adjective: *The painting was **beautiful***. (SVC)
- Adjectival phrase: *The decorators painted the room **bright pink***. (SVOC)
- Noun: *My father was **chairman***. (SVC)
- Noun phrase: *He became **my teacher***. (SVC)
- Clause: *I believed her **to be telling the truth***. (SVOC)

Complements need to be used with a particular group of verbs, which are often referred to as 'link' verbs or copulas. The verbs that can most commonly be used as link verbs are *be, seem, appear (look), feel, get, keep, become, turn*. Often the verbs that describe senses (*look, smell, sound, taste, feel*) can be used as link verbs.

If pupils know verbs as 'doing words', these link verbs are often the ones they have difficulty with, as it is harder to understand that they 'do' anything. They more commonly express a state of being. Therefore, it is best to use the correct terminology 'verb' with pupils from the start.

Finite and non-finite verbs to create subordinate clauses

English sentences should contain a finite verb. A finite verb shows tense and, if it is in the present tense, shows number and person (also with past tense *be*).

If the present or past participles are used on their own, they are non-finite verbs. For example:

- *Looking, screaming, cooking, singing* – present participles
- *Looked, screamed, woken, sung, bought* – past participles (the last three from irregular verbs).

Past participles are easy to confuse with the simple past tense. Regular verbs have the same spelling, using the *-ed* suffix, but there is a difference with some irregular verbs: *woke/woken; sang/sung*. However, when used as a non-finite verb, the subject is rarely included.

Clauses that contain non-finite verbs are called non-finite clauses. They cannot be the main clause in a sentence because they do not contain a finite verb. The non-finite clause would not make sense if it were used on its own as a simple sentence. Using this method of creating a complex sentence adds variety to writing. Pupils can also experiment with swapping the clauses around for effect (and investigating the correct punctuation to use):

- ***Woken by the thunder****, she got out of bed and shut the window.*
- *He checked his watch for the fifth time,* ***worried by the delay****.*
- ***Shouting at the top of his voice****, he cheered his team on.*
- *They walked home from the theatre together,* ***talking all the way****.*

The final non-finite form we can use to create complex sentences is the infinitive, i.e. the verb preceded by *to*: *to speak*, *to eat*, *to survive*. These cannot be used on their own in sentences, being non-finite verbs, but they can be used to create the subordinate clause.

- ***To become a doctor****, you will need to train for many years.* (Correct non-finite form in the subordinate clause and a finite verb required in the main clause.)

These constructions are extremely useful for encouraging pupils to vary their sentence structure. In effect, the non-finite verb is performing the same function as a conjunction – joining two clauses within a sentence.

Prepositions and prepositional phrases

Prepositions can be used to indicate:

- position (place): *in*, *on*, *at*, *above*, *under*, *by*, *beyond*, *behind*, *among*
- direction (place): *into*, *onto*, *towards*, *off*
- time: *on*, *before*, *after*, *during*, *until*, *since*, *for*
- manner: *in*, *by*, *like*, *with*
- attributes: *with*, *without*, *of*
- accompaniment: *with*
- purpose/reason: *because*, *due to*, *as*

These words enable further information to be added, in the form of a noun or noun phrase, which creates a prepositional phrase.

Preposition	+	noun/noun phrase	indicates
under	+	the deep, blue sea	position
into	+	the woods	direction
at	+	midday	time
on	+	Saturdays	time/frequency
between	+	October and December	time/duration
for	+	three days	time/duration
like	+	an angel	manner
with	+	kindness	manner
without	+	hope	attribute
with	+	my friends	accompaniment
as	+	as an example	purpose/reason
because of	+	the snow	purpose/reason

Prepositional phrases can also indicate the agent after the passive – for example, *by the burglar, with a baseball bat.*

Uses of prepositional phrases:

- Post-modify nouns. They occur after the main noun, but are still part of the noun phrase: *The boy* ***in the bright yellow jumper*** *waved excitedly.*
- Adverbial phrases, for example of manner, place, time, reason: *He swam* ***like a fish****. She flew* ***to the shops****. They arranged to meet* ***by the post office****. The footballer had to rest* ***due to a hamstring injury****.*
- Complements to adjectives or adjectival phrases: *The politician was sorry* ***for his comments****. The girl was delighted* ***with her shiny, new bike****.*
- Phrases using the preposition *than* can also qualify adjectives and enable a comparison: *The hare was quicker* ***than the tortoise****.*

Prepositions can also be used with verbs to create phrasal and prepositional verbs (see *Verbs: phrasal, prepositional and phrasal-prepositional* below).

Subordinate clauses

A subordinate clause is a clause that is not the main clause and cannot stand on its own as a sentence. Use of a subordinate clause will create a complex sentence. In some grammar texts, the subordinate clause is referred to as the dependent clause and the main clause as the independent clause. Sometimes subordinate clauses may start a sentence, be positioned at the end of a sentence or they may be embedded within the sentence.

There are different types of subordinate clause: **adverbial, relative** and **nominal**.

An **adverbial clause** is used to express time, conditional, purpose/reason, result, contrast or manner. This type of clause fills the adverbial slot in a sentence.

Finite adverbial clauses (clauses containing a finite form of the verb) will use a conjunction:

- *The road flooded* ***as it rained****.*
- ***When she laughed****, everyone was surprised.*
- *She looked round* ***because she heard the noise****.*
- ***If you are attending****, please let us know.*

Non-finite adverbial clauses will use an infinitive form of the verb or present/past participles used without auxiliary verbs:

- ***To bake the perfect cake****, you need excellent ingredients.*
- *The beacon will shine* ***to warn any travellers****.*
- ***Singing like angels****, the choir sounded heavenly.*
- *The dog trembled,* ***frightened by the thunder****.*

If the subordinate clause starts the sentence, a comma is required to demarcate the two clauses. If the main clause starts the sentence, the comma is optional. Pupils should consider whether it is needed to aid clarity and sense for their reader.

As can be seen above, adverbial clauses can start a sentence or be placed in final position. They can also be embedded, in which case they should be contained within commas. If this additional information is removed, the sentence will still make sense.

- *She could,* ***when she put her mind to it****, do well in most things.*
- *The dog,* ***frightened by the thunder****, trembled.*

A **relative clause** gives extra information about a person, thing or place, or defines exactly which person or thing is being talked about. It comes immediately after a noun (so forms part of the noun phrase) and needs a main clause to make a complete sentence. When the clause adds information, it is enclosed in commas; when it defines or identifies the main noun, commas should not be used.

- *The girl* ***who is standing in the corner of the playground*** *is called Sue.*
- *The man* ***who was playing the trumpet*** *stopped for a moment.*
- *The kitten,* ***which was black and white****, was stuck in the tree.*
- *She was married to an Italian* ***whom she had met on holiday****.*
- *The idea* ***that really grabbed*** *me was to write a poster.*

The above examples use finite verbs, but sometimes the relative pronoun and verb can be omitted to make a non-finite relative clause:

- *The girl* ***standing in the corner of the playground*** *is called Sue.*
- *The man* ***playing the trumpet*** *stopped for a moment.*

Relative clauses form part of the noun phrase; if the noun phrase is being substituted by a pronoun, the whole phrase – including the relative clause – needs to be substituted.

- ***The girl who is standing in the corner of the playground*** *is called Sue.*
- ***She*** *is called Sue.*

Because relative clauses follow a noun and are part of the noun phrase, they are often embedded in a sentence. However, they can also occur in other positions:

- *The man* ***who was playing the trumpet*** *stopped for a moment.* (The noun phrase containing the relative clause is in the subject position in the sentence, so the relative clause is embedded inside the sentence.)
- *She was married to an Italian* ***whom she had met on holiday****.* (The noun phrase containing the relative clause is in the object position, so the relative clause is at the end of the sentence.)

A **nominal clause** fills the subject or object slot in a sentence:

- *I asked her* ***why she had come****.*
- *He felt* ***that he needed to leave****.*
- *She told her mother* ***she would be late home****.*
- ***That she was angry*** *was obvious.*
- ***How the album will do*** *depends on the fans.*

Although nominal clauses are not taught specifically at primary level, it is useful for teachers to be aware of them, since pupils will use these structures in their writing (particularly in reported speech) and will come across them in texts. Many of these start with *that* (a conjunction given in the Year 2 grammar appendix of the National Curriculum). If pupils use *that* in a nominal clause, they will not be able to manipulate the clauses in the same way they do with adverbial clauses. Knowing the difference between adverbial and nominal clauses will help a teacher unpick any confusion.

- *He said that he didn't care.* (SVO with a nominal clause filling the object position.)
- *That he didn't care he said.* (Moving the clause does not leave a structure which makes sense.)

When *that* is used in an adverbial clause it is usually as part of a phrase – for example, *so that, in order that, providing that.*

Subjunctive

Verbs in the subjunctive mood are used to show expression of a hypothetical situation or one where something is demanded, recommended, wished or expected. The following examples show some of the different structures that can be used for the subjunctive mood.

1 *If I **were** to leave, I would miss the final speech*. (subordinate *if* clause expressing a hypothetical situation)
2 *The directors recommend that he **attend** the hearing*. (subordinate *that* clause containing base infinitive form of the verb)
3 *The directors recommend that he **not attend** the hearing*. (subordinate *that* clause containing negative + base infinitive form of the verb)
4 *I would suggest that you **be** ready for the changes*. (subordinate *that* clause containing base infinitive form of the verb *to be*)
5 *It is important that staff **be waiting** outside for their arrival*. (subordinate *that* clause containing continuous form)
6 *They expect that the work **be completed** by Friday*. (subordinate *that* clause containing passive form)

1 *If I **were** to leave, I would miss the final speech.*

The subjunctive mood can be used in subordinate clauses introduced by *if*, which express a hypothetical situation. In these structures, the first and third person singular past form *was* is changed to *were*: *If he **were** a better swimmer, he would have won the race.*

2 *The directors recommend that he **attend** the hearing.*

The subjunctive can be used to express obligation, requirement, desire or compulsion when the sentence contains a subordinate (nominal) clause introduced by *that*. To structure the subjunctive in these situations, the third person singular verb does not take the s suffix. This is the same form as the base infinitive of the verb, i.e. *to attend* would be the infinitive form; the base infinitive form does not include the word *to*.

- *The headmaster requested that the boy **change** his attitude.*
- *The H&S Officer recommended that the manager **reconsider** the advice he gives.*

3 *The directors recommend that he **not attend** the hearing.*

The structures explained in example 2 can also be formed in the negative.

4 *I would suggest that you **be** ready for the changes.*

Again, this is a subordinate *that* clause that uses the base infinitive form of the verb. Pupils will probably only have come across *be* used on its own in a verb position when they are forming a command (*Be ready at three!*). They may not even recognise that *be* is related to *was* and *were*, so using this verb in subjunctive mood may require some explanation.

5 *It is important that staff **be waiting** outside for their arrival.*

The continuous form can also be used in the subjunctive, but it is constructed by using the base infinitive *be* with the present participle, rather than the *is/was/are/were* auxiliaries that we normally use with continuous forms.

6 *They expect that the work* ***be completed*** *by Friday.*
In this type of subjunctive construction, when the verb is required in the passive voice, the bare infinitive *be* is again used as the auxiliary verb rather than the more familiar auxiliaries *is/was/are/were*. This sentence could also be written without using the subjunctive:

- *They expect that the work* ***should be completed*** *by Friday.* (modal verb phrase)
- *They expect that the work* ***will be completed*** *by Friday.* (modal verb phrase)
- *They expect the work* ***to be completed*** *by Friday.* (verb phrase formed by infinitive + past participle)

Other examples of passive use of the subjunctive are:

- *The team managers agreed that the match* ***be postponed****.*
- *The judge demanded that the prisoner* ***be removed*** *from court.*

All these examples can be written in ways that do not use the subjunctive. Modern English has a wide range of modal auxiliary verbs that can be used to express hypothetical situations, obligations, desires and recommendations, so use of the subjunctive mood is optional and may sound strange to some people.

We often come across the subjunctive in fixed expressions. The fact that these are fixed shows the length of time they have existed in our language and reinforces the view that the subjunctive mood is slightly archaic. However, it is worth recognising these for what they are, so a few are listed below. Note the use of *that* clauses and bare infinitives, as in the more modern examples above.

- *God* ***save*** *the Queen!*
- ***Be*** *that as it may…*
- *Heaven* ***forbid*** *that…*
- ***Come*** *what may, I will persevere.*

Verbs: phrasal, prepositional and phrasal-prepositional

Prepositions can be added to verbs to create phrasal, prepositional and phrasal-prepositional verb phrases. These create a different meaning to the one the main verb would have on its own.

1 *The eagle took off into the wind.*
2 *The eagle stretched out his talons towards the water.*
3 *Hungrily, the eagle looked for a meal.*
4 *The eagle put up with the wind patiently.*

Each of these verbs (highlighted in red) includes a verb and a preposition. In the last example, there are two prepositions forming part of the verb. However, there are differences in the way these verbs can be used and how they interact with other sentence elements.

The verb in the first sentence is a phrasal verb, which is used intransitively, i.e. it does not take a direct object. We can see that the sentence has the elements:

The eagle	*took off*	*into the wind.*
subject (S)	verb (V)	adverbial (A)

You cannot usually place an adverbial between the verb and the preposition in phrasal verbs. So we could not say *The eagle took into the wind off*.

The second sentence has a transitive phrasal verb. It takes the direct object (Od) *his talons*. We can analyse the elements of this sentence:

The eagle stretched out his talons towards the water.
S V Od A

As with intransitive phrasal verbs, the adverbial phrase cannot be placed between the verb and the preposition: *The eagle stretched towards the water out his talons.*

However, transitive phrasal verbs can be separated by the direct object. So we can manipulate in the following ways, even when a pronoun replaces the noun phrase filling the direct object slot.

- *The eagle stretched his talons out towards the water.*
- *The eagle stretched them out towards the water.*

The third sentence uses a prepositional verb. We can analyse the elements of this sentence:

Hungrily, the eagle looked for a meal.
A S V Od

The direct object in a sentence with a prepositional verb must follow the preposition, so it cannot act in the same way as a phrasal verb, splitting the verb and particle.

- *Hungrily, the eagle looked a meal for.*
- *Hungrily, the eagle looked it for.*

Another difference between prepositional verbs and phrasal verbs is that an adverbial can split the verb and preposition in a preposition verb, even though the direct object cannot do this.

- *The eagle looked hungrily for a meal.*

The fourth sentence is different in that the verb is followed by two prepositions. This is a phrasal-prepositional verb and it is always used transitively as a direct object must follow the prepositional part of this verb.

The eagle put up with the wind patiently.
S V Od A

In a phrasal-prepositional verb, the first preposition is the phrasal part and the second preposition is the prepositional part. The rules stated above about adverbials apply to each part of these verbs. Adverbials cannot usually split the verb from the phrasal preposition, so we can't have *The eagle put patiently up with the wind.*

However, the adverbial can split the phrasal and prepositional elements: *The eagle put up patiently with the wind.*

Likewise, the direct object cannot split the verb; it has to follow the final preposition: *The eagle put up the wind with patiently.*

There is no doubt that the flexibility of English, in enabling prepositions to be used in these types of structures, adds tremendously to the creativity of our language.

English irregular verbs

Modern English retains many irregular (strong) verb forms from earlier usage. This is a list of many of the irregular verbs currently in use. Some irregular verbs have two forms accepted, e.g. burnt/burned.

Base infinitive	Simple past form	Past participle
arise	arose	arisen
awake	awoke	awoken
be	was, were	been
bear	bore	borne
beat	beat	beaten
become	became	become
begin	began	begun
bend	bent	bent
bet	bet	bet
bid	bid	bid
bind	bound	bound
bite	bit	bitten
bleed	bled	bled
blow	blew	blown
break	broke	broken
breed	bred	bred
bring	brought	brought
broadcast	broadcast	broadcast
build	built	built
burn	burned/burnt	burned/burnt
burst	burst	burst
buy	bought	bought
cast	cast	cast
catch	caught	caught
choose	chose	chosen
cling	clung	clung
come	came	come
cost	cost	cost

creep	crept	crept
cut	cut	cut
deal	dealt	dealt
dig	dug	dug
do	did	done
draw	drew	drawn
dream	dreamed/dreamt	dreamed/dreamt
drink	drank	drunk
drive	drove	driven
eat	ate	eaten
fall	fell	fallen
feed	fed	fed
feel	felt	felt
fight	fought	fought
find	found	found
flee	fled	fled
fling	flung	flung
fly	flew	flown
forbid	forbade	forbidden
forget	forgot	forgotten
forgive	forgave	forgiven
forsake	forsook	forsaken
forswear	forswore	forsworn
freeze	froze	frozen
get	got	got
give	gave	given
go	went	gone
grind	ground	ground
grow	grew	grown
hang	hung	hung
have	had	had
hear	heard	heard

hide	hid	hidden
hit	hit	hit
hold	held	held
hurt	hurt	hurt
keep	kept	kept
know	knew	known
lay	laid	laid
lead	led	led
learn	learned/learnt	learned/learnt
leave	left	left
lend	lent	lent
let	let	let
lie	lay	lain
lose	lost	lost
make	made	made
mean	meant	meant
meet	met	met
pay	paid	paid
put	put	put
quit	quit	quit
read	read	read
rend	rent	rent
ride	rode	ridden
ring	rang	rung
rise	rose	risen
run	ran	run
saw	sawed	sawn
say	said	said
see	saw	seen
seek	sought	sought
sell	sold	sold
send	sent	sent

set	set	set
sew	sewed	sewn
shake	shook	shaken
shed	shed	shed
shine	shone	shone
shoe	shod	shod
shoot	shot	shot
show	showed	shown
shrink	shrank	shrunk
shut	shut	shut
sing	sang	sung
sink	sank	sunk
sit	sat	sat
slay	slew	slain
sleep	slept	slept
slide	slid	slid
sling	slung	slung
slink	slunk	slunk
sow	sowed	sown
speak	spoke	spoken
spend	spent	spent
spin	spun	spun
spread	spread	spread
spring	sprang	sprung
stand	stood	stood
steal	stole	stolen
stick	stuck	stuck
sting	stung	stung
stink	stank	stunk
strew	strewed	strewn
stride	strode	stridden
strike	struck	struck

string	strung	strung
strive	strove	striven
swear	swore	sworn
sweep	swept	swept
swim	swam	swum
take	took	taken
teach	taught	taught
tear	tore	torn
tell	told	told
think	thought	thought
throw	threw	thrown
thrust	thrust	thrust
tread	trod	trodden
understand	understood	understood
wake	woke	woken
wear	wore	worn
weep	wept	wept
win	won	won
wind	wound	wound
wring	wrung	wrung
write	wrote	written

-*ly* adverbs		
angrily	anxiously	awkwardly
badly	boldly	bravely
brightly	carefully	cheerfully
crazily	daily	defiantly
devotedly	dramatically	eagerly
enormously	evenly	eventually
exactly	faithfully	finally
foolishly	fortunately	freely
frequently	gleefully	gracefully
happily	hastily	honestly
hopelessly	hourly	hungrily
innocently	inquisitively	irritably
jealously	kindly	lazily
loosely	madly	merrily
mysteriously	nervously	obediently
occasionally	only	perfectly
politely	poorly	powerfully
promptly	quickly	rapidly
rarely	regularly	rudely
safely	selfishly	seriously
shakily	sharply	silently
slowly	solemnly	speedily
sternly	tightly	unexpectedly
usually	warmly	weakly
wearily	weekly	wildly

Some adverbs that can be used to pre-modify adjectives		
absolutely	almost	awfully
badly	completely	considerably
dearly	deeply	drastically
dreadfully	enormously	entirely
especially	exceedingly	extraordinarily
extremely	fairly	fully
greatly	hard	hugely
immensely	incredibly	just
largely	massively	moderately
nearly	noticeably	partly
perfectly	poorly	positively
powerfully	practically	pretty
purely	quite	rather
really	reasonably	remarkably
significantly	simply	slightly
strongly	sufficiently	surprisingly
terribly	totally	tremendously
truly	unbelievably	understandably
utterly	very	wonderfully